Pretty & Organized

JANE HUGHES

Pretty & Organized

GO CLUTTER-FREE
WITH 30 EASY-TO-MAKE
DECORATIVE STORAGE IDEAS
FOR EVERY ROOM IN YOUR HOME

FIREFLY BOOKS

A FIREFLY BOOK

Published by Firefly Books Ltd, 2015

Copyright © 2015 Quintet Publishing

First printing

**Publisher Cataloging-in-Publication Data
(U.S.)**

A CIP record for this title is available from
the Library of Congress

**Library and Archives Canada
Cataloguing in Publication**

A CIP record for this title is available from
Library and Archives Canada

Published in the United States by
Firefly Books (U.S.) Inc.
P.O. Box 1338, Ellicott Station
Buffalo, New York 14205

Published in Canada by
Firefly Books Ltd.
50 Staples Avenue, Unit 1
Richmond Hill, Ontario L4B 0A7

Printed in China

Conceived, designed, and produced by
Quintet Publishing
Project Editor: Caroline Elliker
Designer: Bonnie Bryan
Photographer: Sussie Bell
Art Director: Michael Charles
Editorial Director: Emma Bastow
Publisher: Mark Searle

CONTENTS

Tidy Bags on page 27

INTRODUCTION

If you've picked up this book, the chances are you feel the need to organize and declutter your living space. The problems of storage are universal. Whether you live in a large, airy house, a tiny apartment, or an old farmhouse, most of us don't have enough space for the things we own. A lot of this can be attributed to the psychology of the times we live in. Go back a mere 60 years, before the advent of shopping malls and giant supermarkets, and our buying habits were much more functional. Shops were smaller and our choices were fewer. Cars were still seen as luxuries. All of this meant that we bought only what we really needed, and in quantities that we could manage to carry home.

Now, however, we live in a highly consumerist age, driven by aspiration and the idea that everything we desire is obtainable. It's easy to buy stuff if you have the means. And it follows that, as our lives and our minds become busier and faster, they also become more cluttered. All of which makes the idea of simple, organized living ever more appealing.

Fads and trends may come and go, but a tidier home is something you will always benefit from. And although a more minimal approach isn't always easy and may not be for everyone, the benefits of a clutter-free space with simple storage for belongings will help declutter your head too. Need proof? According to recent studies carried out by the American Cleaning Institute, removing excess clutter could reduce housework in the average home by 40 percent. It's worth bearing in mind too that according to *Time Magazine*, household dust contains—among other things—human skin, decomposing insects, food debris, and sometimes even lead, arsenic and pesticides. On that note, now might be a good time to say goodbye, to those dusty old trinkets or that pile of magazines and papers you think might one day come in handy, but you know you're never going to look at again. Learn how to let go of possessions that you no longer need, and be ruthless.

Being organized isn't something you do when you have a bit of spare time. It's a daily, weekly, life-long job, and as things change or evolve in your life, you may have to adapt your ideas to fit. Being able to quickly lay your hands on an unpaid bill or school permission slip can save a lot of time and stress. Consider using a household journal containing a calendar to hold all your important information and dates, as well as contact details, school or work information, shopping lists, and bills. You can make your own from a ring binder and paper or work from a notebook. It may be that you find a wall planner, hung in a visible place, works better for you.

Here are examples of some basic hassle-free storage solutions:

- Keep items in transparent containers to enable you to find them easily. The more accessible the storage location, the better.

- Make it a rule to sort through clothes, shoes, and accessories each season. Get rid of any unwanted items, and if they're still wearable put them in a goodwill donation bag and move them out before you change your mind.

- Put labels on everything. Having tins and boxes for storage is great for a neat look, but not when you don't have a clue as to what's inside any of them. A label maker is a good investment, although if you have nice writing and a decent pen you can make some with pretty sticky labels. Chalkboard stickers are a good idea if you are changing the contents regularly.

Throughout this book you'll find more handy tips on how to tidy and organize things in stylish ways that complement your home. You will also find 30 projects that you can make for your home, designed to make life easier and simpler while remaining aesthetically pleasing. These easy-to-follow projects range far and wide, from pretty shelves and mail baskets to toy storage and meal planners. Where templates are provided, please note these will need photocopying and resizing according to the scale given.

All in all, this book offers practical solutions to practical problems. Not only will your home feel like a better space to live in, it should be nicer to look at. None of these projects will take up hours of your life or tug hard on your purse strings, and they're designed for anyone and everyone. A well-organized home can have a big effect on your own well-being, and the benefits are for the long term. What's more, it also leaves you free to get on with the things in life that you really want to do.

Enjoy!

Garment Bags on page 89

FOUR STAGES OF ORGANIZED STORAGE

There are four main processes involved in achieving a pretty and organized home:

(1) DECLUTTER

Everyone needs to cut back on the clutter at some point in their life, although it's not always obvious how to go about it. Tackling the whole house can be overwhelming, so the first thing to do is make a list of the spaces that need work. Plan a realistic schedule and make notes on ideas that could make the spaces work better for you. Check back to your list often and tick off the jobs you have done.

(2) SORT

To make the job of decluttering easier you will need four bags or boxes. Label them "Keep," "Donate," "Recycle," and "Garbage." Use these bags for every area you work on. Choose a day or time when you will be uninterrupted to make sure you can finish what you started. Begin with your first room and start filling the bags, and if there is anything you are unsure of put that in a separate pile. Revisit this unsure pile when you have cleared the room and have an overall idea of what's staying and going. You may decide that rather than find a place for these items you can say goodbye to them, too.

Be ruthless. At some point the room will look like it has been raided, but it will look worse before it looks better, so don't give up. For items you want to keep but don't use every day, consider storage such as a loft, attic or basement. Use strong boxes or bags that will keep your possessions dry and clean, and label them clearly.

Useful items you can gather in preparation are strong boxes, large zipped bags, sticky labels or luggage tags, some good music and a camera for some before and after shots—always good for a bit of motivational inspiration!

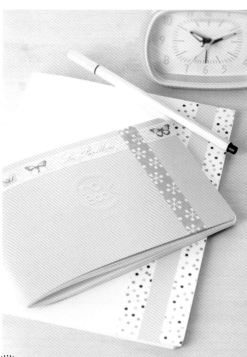

1

Tackle one room at a time and be realistic with your schedule.

Labels are crucial when sorting your belongings. Not only will they help you locate items quickly, but they will also add a personal touch as well as a sophisticated style to your containers.

③ CLEAN

Once your room is cleared, give it a really good clean. Have all your cleaning products on hand. Start at the top and work downward, dusting on top of shelves and behind curtains. Wash any soft furnishings and wipe down any areas that don't get seen very often. Finally, vacuum or clean the floor. Be prepared to do this area again when you have finished putting everything back! Now your space is all clean and ready for the next step.

④ ORGANIZE

Think about how you can organize the things you are putting back. Make a list of any items you will need, like files or boxes, and put them straight to work. Don't put anything back in the room unless it has a designated place. If you are going to have a system for where things go, make sure all house members are aware and that they work with you to keep the room tidy and organized. It's easier said than done, but you can try.

③

It's worth spending some extra time cleaning your storage space before you begin organizing it. Using attractive, personalized equipment will make the job more enjoyable.

A good tip to keep your space clear and tidy after all your hard work is to spend 10 minutes every day putting everything away and ensuring each item is clearly labeled.

PROJECT SELECTOR

Entrance

20 Shoe Storage

22 Mail Basket

27 Tidy Bags

32 Coat Pegs

Living Room

62 Magazine Holders

63 Storage Tubs

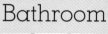

67 Storage Cart

Kitchen & Utility Room

41 Cutlery Holder

42 Magnetic Tins

45 Meal Planner

48 Food Covers

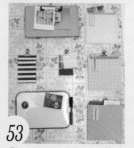

53 Cupboard Door Organizer

Bathroom

73 Towel Roller

76 First Aid Tin

Bedroom

Kids' Room

Home Office & Craft Room

Outdoors

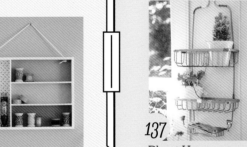

Chapter 1

ENTRANCE

First appearances make a big impression. The entrance to your home is a taste of what's to come, so don't fall at the first hurdle with messy floors and piles of unopened mail. Impress visitors by creating a clean, spacious environment that will instantly put them at ease and welcome them in.

ENTRANCE

It's the first place you see when you walk in to your home so you want it to feel open and inviting. You will probably need a place to store shoes and coats as well as scarves and bags, and if possible somewhere to sit. A good idea is to hang a peg rail by the door with bags for smaller things like gloves or hats or daily school items. Hang chalkboard on the back of the door to note down any reminders that will catch your eye before you leave the house. A wall-mounted mail basket or shelf is good for catching incoming and outgoing mail.

A tall bookcase can be customized by removing a few of the higher shelves and adding coat pegs. Use the lower shelves for extra storage with labeled baskets. Keep the floor clear by encouraging everyone to put their shoes away as soon as they walk through the door. Store less frequently used shoes and seasonal coats in your closet to free up more space.

The back of a door can be used as extra storage for bags by adding a few hooks. If you have children, add some lower down so they can be encouraged to hang up their own things. Keep a basket by the front door. Fill it with things like a clothes brush or lint rollers, hairbrush, and a mirror for a last-minute inspection as you leave the house.

Mail Basket on page 22

Tidy Bags on page 27

Shoe Storage

This is a re-purposing project that can turn some drawers into handy shoe storage. You will need to find a chest with two or three drawers, preferably with legs, although this is not essential. The drawers need to be the type that are set on side runners, so when you remove them you have an open space rather than shelves. The curtain hides the shoes and keeps it looking pretty; it hangs on a plastic-coated curtain wire attached by hooks. Inside I have used shelf risers used in kitchen cupboards. They double up the storage space and are metal for easy cleaning.

TOOLS & MATERIALS

- A wooden chest of drawers with legs if possible, 2–3 drawers maximum
- Sandpaper
- Paint—main color plus extra if you are painting the legs
- Paintbrush
- Masking tape
- Plastic-coated curtain wire—measure the chest for an idea of how much you will need

- 2 small hooks and eyes
- Wire cutters
- Fabric—measure the gap at the front of the drawers and add extra for seam allowances
- Tape measure
- Sewing machine
- Thread
- Pins
- Scissors

To make the shoe storage

1. Remove the drawers and put to one side. Make sure the surfaces are clean and dry, then sand lightly to allow adhesion of the paint.
2. Paint the inside and outside of the chest. Apply a couple of coats for an even finish.
3. Allow to dry thoroughly.
4. I chose some white and pink fabric for the curtains so I wanted to add some of this color to the painted legs. If your unit has legs and you wish to do this, then carefully turn the chest upside down and mask off the parts you are going to paint. Apply the colors and allow to dry.

To make the curtain

5. Measure the open part at the front of the chest. Add an extra 5½ inch (14 cm) to the width and 3¼ inch (8 cm) to the height for the seam allowance and for the channel along the top to hold the wire. Use these measurements to cut the fabric to size. Fold over twice, press the two side hems and stitch.

6. Take the top hem and fold over twice to form a ¾ inch (2 cm) channel. Iron, pin and stitch down. Measure and mark with pins the length you want the curtain to be. The one shown here is the same length as the open front. Fold over twice, press and stitch down to hem. Press the curtain.

7. Add the eye hooks to the outer edges of the chest, measure the distance between the two hooks and take off 1¼ inch (4 cm). The wire is slightly stretchy; you need it to be a little shorter than the actual length to keep it taut. Using the wire cutters, cut the curtain wire to that measurement and add the hooks to either end. Thread the curtain wire through the channel and hang in place.

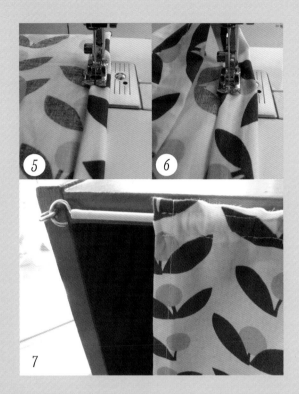

Tips

- You could turn this into a little seat by adding a cushion on top, and if you place a metal tray on the floor underneath you can sit muddy boots in there to dry.

- If you prefer not to have the curtain you could find a large basket that fits in the opening and put the shoes inside.

- If you don't have legs on your drawers then you could add casters.

- This project works well for other rooms too. You could remove some drawers from a unit to store toys in a playroom, or it would make a good record player stand with vinyl storage underneath. If you keep the drawers from this DIY you could add casters to the bottom and use them for under-bed storage.

Mail Basket

This basket is ideal for holding all your correspondence. Hang it on the wall by the front door as a reminder to mail out birthday cards or hand in school permission slips. It has an industrial feel, but the liner softens the look and gives it a neater finish. If you make a few you could have one for each house member and they look great all hanging in a row. You will need to find some galvanized mesh, like the kind you would use to make small animal runs. Try to find some that isn't too tough as you need to be able to cut and bend it. It can be bought in sheets or on rolls from garden centers or hardware stores, and one sheet should be enough to make one basket.

TOOLS & MATERIALS

- Galvanized wire mesh sheet, no smaller than 31½ x 23½ inch (80 x 59.5 cm)
- Wire cutters
- Pliers
- Metal ruler
- Pencil
- Black paint spray (optional)
- Fabric for the outer, no smaller than 31½ x 23½ inch (80 x 59.5 cm)

- Plain fabric for the liner, no smaller than 31½ x 23½ inch (80 x 59.5 cm)
- Scissors
- Sewing machine
- Thread
- Iron
- Pins
- Metal label holder
- Double-sided foam tape

To make the basket

1. Lay the mesh out on a flat surface. Using a photocopier, enlarge the template opposite and place it on the mesh. Cut out the shape with wire cutters. As you cut, make sure to leave as much of the wire ends as possible as they will be used to bend around and hold the sides together.

2. Using the metal ruler, bend in the sides and fold up the base and front until you are happy with the shape.

3. Using the pliers, bend the ends of the cut wire around to hold the folded sides and base in place.

4. This part is a bit tricky and you may get scratched. Try it with protective gloves if preferred. Continue neatly bending in the ends until they are all done. At this point I sprayed the basket with a black enamel spray to give it a more vintage feel. If you do this, spray outside in a well-ventilated area and allow it to dry.

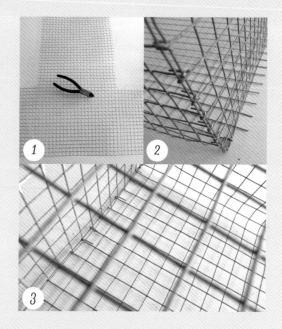

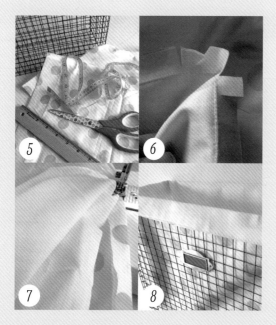

To make the liner

5. Using basket liner templates as a guide, mark out the shapes onto the fabric and cut out.

6. Make the outer bag first by taking the front piece and the long piece, placing them right sides together and sew down the side, along the base and up the other side, leaving a ⅜ inch (1 cm) seam. When you get to the corners stop with the needle in the fabric, lift up the machine foot and carefully turn the fabric 45 degrees. Make sure the fabric is flat and continue to the next corner and repeat. When finished, snip into the corners to help the fabric sit neatly.

7. Repeat the same process with the back piece. Press and turn the right way out. Sew the lining fabric together in the same way but leave this one inside out and place inside the outer bag. Fold and press down the top hem of both bags and sew together close to the edge. Place inside the basket and fold down the top over the outside.

8. Add a metal label holder with a piece of double-sided foam tape. You can now hang the basket by adding a couple of picture hooks to the wall.

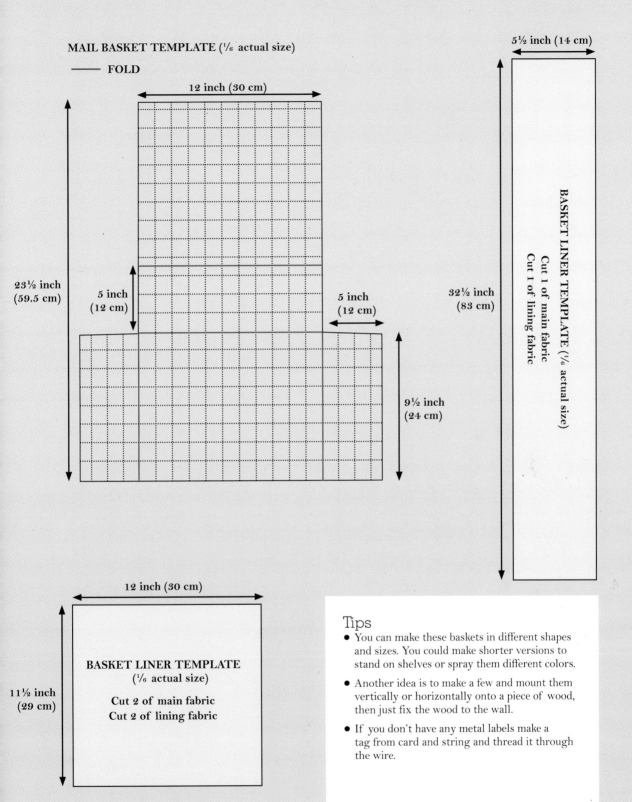

MAIL BASKET TEMPLATE (¹⁄₆ actual size)

—— **FOLD**

12 inch (30 cm)

23½ inch (59.5 cm)

5 inch (12 cm)

5 inch (12 cm)

9½ inch (24 cm)

5½ inch (14 cm)

BASKET LINER TEMPLATE (¹⁄₆ actual size)

Cut 1 of main fabric
Cut 1 of lining fabric

32½ inch (83 cm)

12 inch (30 cm)

BASKET LINER TEMPLATE
(¹⁄₆ actual size)

Cut 2 of main fabric
Cut 2 of lining fabric

11½ inch (29 cm)

Tips
- You can make these baskets in different shapes and sizes. You could make shorter versions to stand on shelves or spray them different colors.

- Another idea is to make a few and mount them vertically or horizontally onto a piece of wood, then just fix the wood to the wall.

- If you don't have any metal labels make a tag from card and string and thread it through the wire.

Tidy Bags

These handy bags for hanging in your hall or entryway are ideal for keeping hats and scarves in, or things for school or work. Each bag has the initials of each house member on it so that everyone can keep their own items tidied away inside. The bags are made from medium-weight fabric and are lined with plain white cotton. The letters are painted on using a washable neon fabric paint. The drawstring used on these bags is like a very strong shoelace-type cord and I found the best selection in online camping and sailing sites.

TOOLS & MATERIALS (for a standard-sized pump bag)

- 31½ x 23¾ inch (80 x 60 cm) piece of medium-weight cotton fabric
- 31½ x 19¾ inch (80 x 50 cm) piece of white cotton fabric
- 10½ foot (3.2 m) length of $^1/_{64}$ format inch (0.4 cm) wide drawstring
- Fabric paint
- Paintbrush
- Adhesive letters

- Scissors/Craft knife
- Masking tape
- Sheet of paper
- Sewing machine
- Sewing thread
- Safety pin
- Iron
- Plain handkerchief

To make the outer bag

1. Enlarge the templates on page 31 using a photocopier, to make paper pattern pieces. The measurements used here are 14½ x 18½ inch (37 x 47 cm) for the main pieces, and 14½ x 3¼ inch (37 x 8 cm) for the two drawstring channel pieces. With your paper patterns, mark out the main fabric pieces and lining pieces and carefully cut them out.

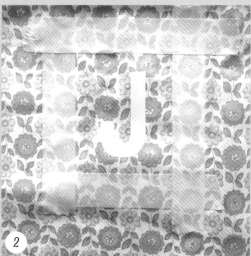

Printing the letters

2. Take the front piece of the main bag and position your chosen letter sticker in the center. Mark out a square around the letter with masking tape to mask off the areas to paint.

3. Place a piece of paper underneath the fabric to stop the paint going through the fabric. Neatly apply the fabric paint onto the fabric inside the square. Allow the paint to dry before peeling off the sticker and tape. Place the handkerchief over the print and iron the area on a medium to high setting to seal the paint.

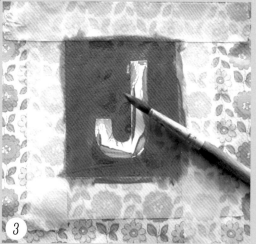

To make the drawstring loops

4. Cut a strip of the main fabric measuring 1¼ x 6¼ inch (3 x 16 cm), neatly fold in and hide the raw edges along the length of the strip, press and sew down to make a narrow strip. Cut in half so you have two pieces; fold each of them in half and pin to the front piece of the bag 1½ inch (4 cm) up from the base on each side with the folded edge facing inwards.

To make the bag

5. Take the two main bag pieces and place the right sides together. Sew along the sides and bottom with a ⅜ inch (1 cm) seam, and backstitch when you sew over the two loops to secure.

6. Leave the top edge open. Take the white lining pieces and sew together in the same way.

7. Turn the main bag the right way round but leave the lining inside out and place inside the main bag.

8. Fold over and pin the top hem of the inner and lining. Stitch down close to the edge.

To make the drawstring channel

9. Take one of the channel pieces and zigzag stitch along the raw edges to prevent fraying.

10. Using the iron, fold and press all the edges in ⅜ inch (1 cm). Fold in half and press flat. Repeat with the other piece.

11. Pin the folded channels to the top opening, making sure they sit just below the top of the bag.

12. Sew a row of stitching along each channel to attach.

13. Cut the drawstring in half. Attach the safety pin to one end and thread through the channel going through both sides.

14. Pull the string so it is evenly distributed and thread one piece through the loop at the base and tie in a secure knot. Repeat with the other length of drawstring.

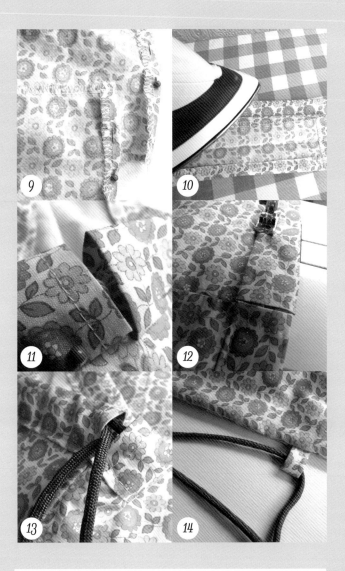

Tips

- For a simpler version you could just buy drawstring bags and paint the initials on. You could leave out the loop and just have the drawstring at the top.

- You could make these bags for bedrooms too, or use them for laundry, making one for dark colors and one for whites to make washing and sorting easier.

TIDY BAG TEMPLATES (⅓ actual size)

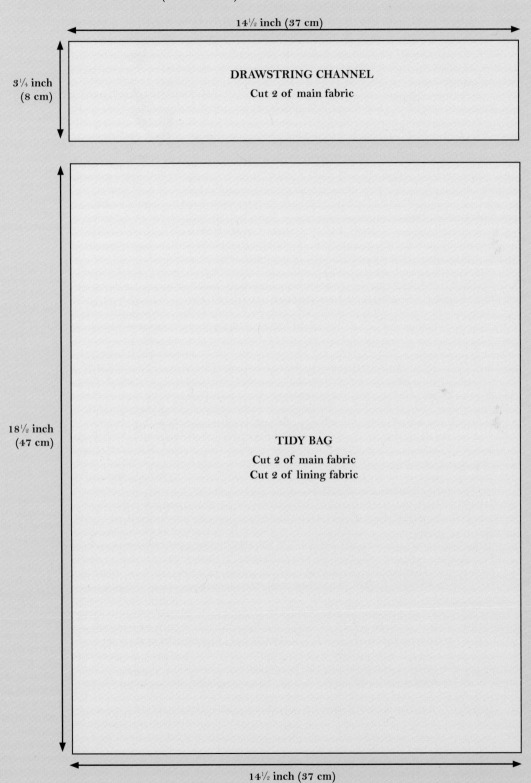

14½ inch (37 cm)

DRAWSTRING CHANNEL
Cut 2 of main fabric

3¼ inch
(8 cm)

18½ inch
(47 cm)

TIDY BAG

Cut 2 of main fabric
Cut 2 of lining fabric

14½ inch (37 cm)

Coat Pegs

This peg rail is a simple and pretty way to keep the hall space tidy. Just as at school, giving a name to a peg can help keep things in order. Using reclaimed wood and some pretty hooks, it is a simple project but one that can be made to fit your home and style. If you can't find hooks in different colors, paint your own using a good acrylic paint with a topcoat of varnish. Make sure the wall you attach this to is strong enough to hold the weight of a few coats and bags. Decide where you would like to hang the rail and work off the measurements of the space you have.

TOOLS & MATERIALS

- A length of 1 inch (2.5 cm) thick wood measuring 33½ x 8 inch (85 x 20.5 cm). I have used a piece of old baseboard as it was just the right size.
- Sandpaper
- Woodfiller (if needed)
- Paint
- Paintbrush
- Ruler or tape measure
- Pencil
- 6 coat hooks in different sizes and colors
- Screwdriver and screws
- 6 metal label holders
- 2 wall plates for attaching to the wall

1. Start by sanding and preparing the wood, filling any holes or gaps to ensure you have a smooth surface. Paint the wood in your chosen color. Apply several coats for an even finish and allow to dry overnight.

2. Using a ruler and pencil, measure and mark where you would like the six hooks to be.

3. Using the screws, attach the hooks securely. Add the label plates with small screws or pins directly above each hook.

4. Attach the wall plates to the back and fix securely to the wall. Insert labels into holders as required.

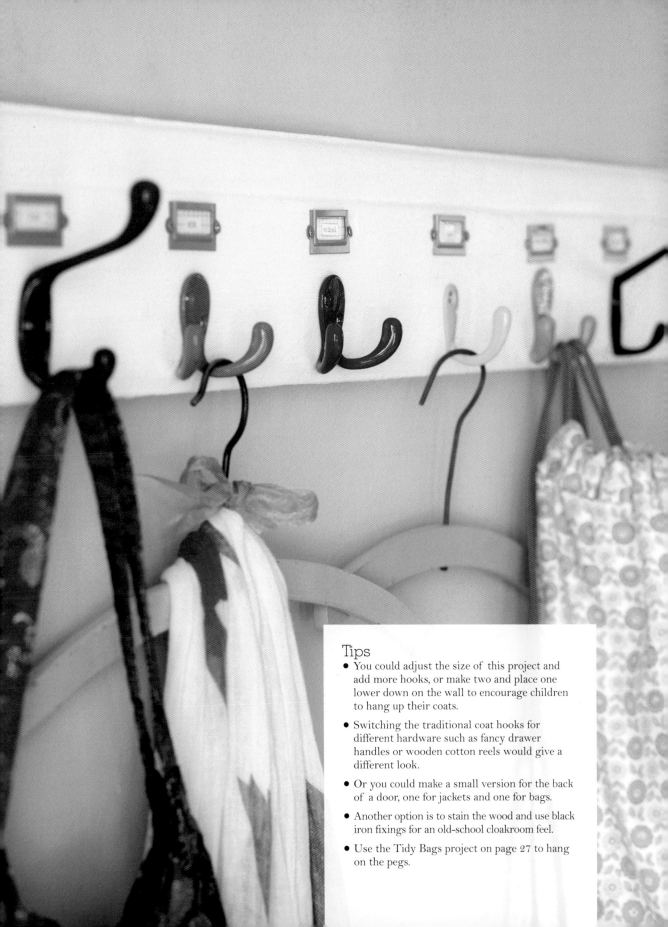

Tips

- You could adjust the size of this project and add more hooks, or make two and place one lower down on the wall to encourage children to hang up their coats.

- Switching the traditional coat hooks for different hardware such as fancy drawer handles or wooden cotton reels would give a different look.

- Or you could make a small version for the back of a door, one for jackets and one for bags.

- Another option is to stain the wood and use black iron fixings for an old-school cloakroom feel.

- Use the Tidy Bags project on page 27 to hang on the pegs.

Further Ideas

This customized bureau has been painted to match the entranceway color scheme. The little drawers are useful for small objects such as keys and mail.

Tip
Next time you enter your home, take some time to think about the first impressions any visitor will experience, and ask yourself what can be improved upon.

Tip
Entranceways often end up as dumping grounds for indoor and outdoor clutter. Ask yourself how often you actually use these items!

Paint a wooden hanger and add shower curtain rings for a place to hang scarves and accessories.

Hide away your ugly cleaning equipment inside an attractive curtained closet. You'll be surprised how much you can fit in the corners of your entrance area.

Chapter 2

KITCHEN & UTILITY ROOM

There are lots of practical and easy ways to make the best use of this busy space. Prevent chaos and save time by making good use of hidden memo boards and nifty food storage techniques that everyone in the household will thank you for.

KITCHEN & UTILITY ROOM

In the majority of homes, the kitchen is the busiest and most used room. Storage and organization is key to making the kitchen do all its jobs efficiently. Regularly going through cupboards, pantries and fridges helps keep the shelves from bending under the strain of out-of-date foods. Think about using things like shelf risers to add more space and group objects together that you use regularly. Put less-used items in baskets on higher shelves so they are easier to pull out. Keep a foldaway stool handy so you can reach them. Plastic baskets can organize your food purchases in the fridge and freezer too. For example, use a basket to store packed lunch supplies or fresh fruit in the fridge.

Hide appliances or open shelving with pretty handmade curtains, and use hooks under shelves to add storage space for cups. Keep work surfaces free from clutter by using a letter rack for correspondence and sort through it regularly. Meal planners and shopping lists help with budgeting for weekly shops and also mean you can delegate the cooking. The inside of cupboard doors can be useful for holding hidden notice boards and reminders.

However tempting, try not to over buy on plates and mugs; have as many as you need plus a few extra for guests. Use the "one in, one out" system to keep the shelves from overflowing. Add dividers or cutlery trays to drawers and only keep what you need in them. Store spare bulbs, fuses and batteries in a clearly labeled basket.

Organize your kitchen layout so it works for you. Keep cups and tea-making supplies near the kettle, regularly used plates and glasses at the front of the cupboards, store bread near the toaster, etc. Have day-to-day items such as cutlery, placemats and napkins by the kitchen table.

Cleaning products don't always come in the best packaging. You could decant them into nice jars and bottles or, even better, make your own products from natural ingredients. Keep a labeled tin handy with useful stain removers and prewash soaps. Fill a jar with spare buttons and a mending kit for emergency repairs. Save old tins or boxes and customize them to make pretty storage for shoe shine kits or first aid. Metal pails are good for storing cleaning equipment and mean you can easily move your supplies from room to room. Think about using labeled laundry bags for whites and colors to save sorting through them on washday.

A shelf with a rail underneath can be used to hang clothes straight from the dryer or line. Open shelves work well, so long as you contain everything in baskets or boxes to keep it looking neat. Just adding simple details like a pretty ironing board cover can make a big difference.

Invites

Receipts

Coupons

Cupboard Door Organizer on page 53

Cutlery Holder

This holder is really useful to keep on your dining or kitchen table, and as it has a handle you can easily carry it from table to kitchen or outside for backyard dining. The holder is a wooden box planter, like the ones used for herbs on kitchen windowsills, and can be found in garden supply stores. The re-used jars are standard size, but I chose ones of different heights and added some more decorative ones.

TOOLS & MATERIALS

- A wooden box
- White paint
- Black paint
- Paintbrush
- Sandpaper
- Paper plate
- Sponge brush or small paintbrush
- 4 glass jars or more if you can fit them in
- Dot stickers in various colors

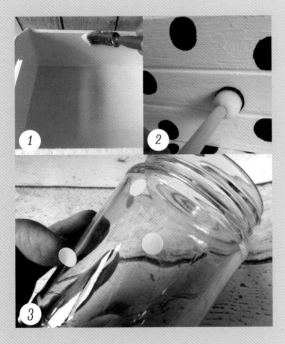

1. Sand down the box ready to paint. Paint the whole thing inside and out in the white paint. Leave to dry and add a second coat if needed.
2. Put some black paint on a paper plate and, using the sponge brush, apply the dots. You can just paint them on using a small paintbrush if you prefer. Allow the dots to dry thoroughly.
3. Ensure the jars are clean and dry. Add the sticky dots to the jars in even patterns.

Tips
- Try to match the colors to your tableware for a coordinated look.
- The jars could be switched for condiments or kitchen utensils.

Magnetic Tins

Do you ever buy strange food or teas just because the tins are nice? If so, then this project is for you. The ones you will need to make these magnetic pots should be square-shaped or at least have one flat side so the magnets can be applied. They need to be small or medium in size as the bigger ones will be too heavy to stick when they are filled. The best tins tend to be ones like these tea tins I found in a grocery store, but anything with a good design or color will do. The magnetic strips come in different widths but you can use two or three per tin if they are not wide enough.

TOOLS & MATERIALS

- Tins of various sizes, square-shaped with at least one flat side
- Extra strong self-adhesive magnetic strips
- Scissors
- Ruler

1. Take the empty tin and if it has a lid, remove it. Measure the height and width of the tin.

2. Cut the magnetic strips so that they will cover the entire back of the tin as this will make the magnetic pull stronger. Stick the strips on and press firmly to make sure they are well attached.

Tips
- If you can't find any nice tins then try decorating your own using stickers or paper.
- For a more permanent fixture, the tins can be fixed onto a strip of wood and then screwed to a wall.

Lasagne

Salad

Fish pie

Stew

PIZZA & SALAD
INGREDIENTS:
800g/1¾lb '00' flour
200g/7oz semolina flour, plus extra
1 tsp salt
1 tbsp caster sugar
14g/½oz dried yeast
4 tbsp extra virgin olive oil

2 x 400g/14oz tins San Marzano to
200g/7oz mozzarella cheese
150g/5½oz dolcelatte cheese
100g/3½oz pecorino cheese (or a
3 tbsp olive oil
sea salt and freshly ground black pe
handful basil leaves

2 bunches rocket
75g/2½oz parmesan cheese, shave
3 tbsp olive oil
1 tbsp bals

VEGETARIAN COTTAGE PIE
INGREDIENTS:
500g/1lb 2oz floury potatoes, such as King Edward or Maris Piper, peeled, cut into pieces
300g/10½oz parsnips or swede, peeled, cut into pieces, boiled until tender, drained
knob of butter
splash milk
salt and freshly ground black pepper
1 tbsp rapeseed or groundnut oil
1 onion, peeled, finely chopped
1 garlic clove, peeled, crushed to a paste with the edge of a knife
1 large carrot, peeled, finely chopped
1 leek, trimmed, thinly sliced
2 tsp chopped fresh thyme leaves
300g/10½oz Quorn
1 x 400g/14oz can cannellini beans, drained and rinsed
1 x 400g/14oz can chopped tomatoes
1 tbsp tomato purée
salt and freshly ground black pepper
green vegetables, to serve

Meal Planner

This idea came about because the favorite line in our house around 5 p.m. is, "What's for dinner?" This clipboard planner is made to hang in your kitchen and you can plan your weekly meals, shopping and cooking, keeping all the information in one place. It shows main meals for each day of the week and how to make them. It is made from a wooden clipboard and scrapbooking card and is a really simple DIY project. The planner can be personalized to suit your lifestyle. The labels can be moved around or added to and the recipes are laminated so they stay clean.

TOOLS & MATERIALS

- An 8½ x 11 inch (21.5 x 28 cm) wooden clipboard
- Scrapbooking card
- Sewing machine
- Sewing thread
- Alphabet stickers
- Neon page markers
- White paper
- Printer
- Laminator sheets and laminator
- Scissors
- Pencil
- Double-sided foam tape
- Small colored dot stickers

To cover the clipboard

1. Take a piece of patterned card and place the clipboard on top and draw around it.

2. Carefully cut this shape out with the scissors. The metal clip on this type of board doesn't usually come off so you will need to cut around the shape of the clip. Put double-sided tape on the reverse of the card and stick to the board.

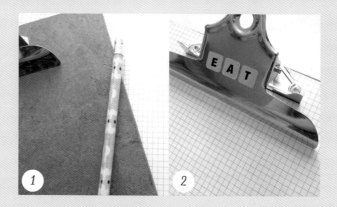

To make the pocket

3. Take two pieces of card. Place the clipboard on top and draw around the bottom half of the board. Cut this shape out, making sure it is only half the height of the clipboard.

4. Take one of the card pieces and cut ⅜ inch (1 cm) from the top edge so that when placed together it will be a little bit shorter. Stitch the two pieces together, leaving the top edge open.

5. Add the double-sided foam tape to the back of the pocket and stick down onto the clipboard.

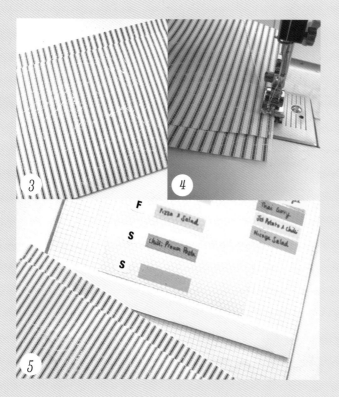

To make the meal planner

6. Cut a piece of card 7¾ x 6 inch (20 x 15 cm), and stick the letters for each day of the week down the left-hand side. Write up your meal ideas and add them to the card.

7. Write extras and keep them over on the right-hand side so you can switch them around. Add stickers for things like vegetarian, gluten free or low calorie, etc. Print out your favorite recipes for your chosen meals as a guide for size so they fit in the pocket. The ones here measure approximately 7¾ x 6 inch (20 x 15 cm). Laminate the recipes so they last longer and put them in the pocket. Decorate the board with the letter stickers and tape.

Tips
- You could use any kind of clipboard for this or you can make your own from a piece of strong card and a large bulldog clip.
- Keep a notebook in the pocket so you can list any supplies needed, and be ready for the next grocery trip. You can store recipes in there too.

Food Covers

These little food covers will fit over cups and bowls, and if you make them
in a few different sizes they can work for all sorts of kitchen items. Use them
instead of aluminum foil or plastic wrap. The traditional ones are made from
thin plastic, but these will last longer and as long as you use easy-care fabrics
they can be washed at a high temperature and re-used. The handy bag
keeps them all together so you can hang it up in a safe place and will always
know where to find them. For this project you need narrow elasticized lace
with a pretty edging and some fabric pieces in various patterns. Look for any
dresses or shirts you may have put in the goodwill bag from your clear-out as
you can re-use the fabric from these.

TOOLS & MATERIALS

- Clean fabric pieces varying in size from
  7 inch (18 cm) square up to 15¾ inch
  (40 cm) square
- Narrow elasticized lace in pretty colors;
  approximately 6½ feet (2 m) should be
  enough to make 6 covers in various sizes
- 11¾ inch (29.5 cm) of bias binding
- Fabric measuring 7¾ x 15¾ inch
  (20 x 40 cm) for the bag

- Sewing machine
- Thread
- Scissors
- Pinking shears
- Large safety pin
- Pins
- Pen/pencil
- Circular objects like plates, bowls, etc.
- Iron

Tips

- If you can't find the lacy type of elastic, you could use the plain narrow kind and sew it in the same way but on the underside of the fabric so it isn't visible when the covers are being used.

- Any fabric will work for this project but lightweight cottons are easiest to clean.

- This DIY is a good way of using up fabric pieces you may have left over from other projects.

- In the summer you can use them to cover food and drinks outdoors to keep the bugs out.

To make the covers

1. Place your fabric on a flat surface, take your circular objects and put them over the fabric so you can trace the shape with a pen.

2. Using the pinking shears to keep the edges neat, cut out the circles before pressing them flat. Note each cover will fit a slightly smaller container.

3. Take the full length of elastic and, using a small running stitch, begin sewing it to your circle, stretching the elastic fully as you go but keeping the fabric flat; this way the elastic gathers the fabric as you sew. Backstitch at the start and finish to secure the elastic in place and cut off the excess.

To make the bag

4. Cut out a rectangle of fabric measuring 7¾ x 15¾ inch (20 x 40 cm), press the fabric and fold in half with right sides facing together. Using a ⅜ inch (1 cm) seam allowance, stitch down the side and bottom of the fabric, leaving the top open. Fold the top hem over twice and pin. Stitch down leaving a ¾ inch (2 cm) gap at the finish to create a channel for threading the binding for the drawstring through.

5. Take the binding, fold in half width-ways and stitch down to make a narrow strip. Attach the safety pin to one end of the binding and begin pushing through the gap and through the channel at the top of the bag, continuing until the safety pin and binding pops out of the gap. Ease the binding out so that both ends are the same length and knot together.

Invites

Receipts

Coupons

Cupboard Door Organizer

A regularly used cupboard door is a great place to hang important memos or reminders, and it's a good way to keep them stored neatly out of sight.
For this project you will need a door that is flat on the inside. First you should check that if you hang anything on the inside of the door it will still close. Choose color schemes and patterns that match the room and try to find coordinating pens or accessories. The envelope pockets are good for keeping receipts or tickets safe, and you could also have one for shopping coupons.

TOOLS & MATERIALS

- A piece of wallpaper big enough to cover the cupboard door
- Mod Podge® or PVA glue
- Medium-sized brush
- Clear varnish (optional)
- Small bulldog clips with holes in the handles
- Small white board and pen
- Small clipboard
- 3 pieces of patterned card measuring 8½ x 15 inch (21.5 x 38 cm)
- Patterned sticky tape
- Small screws and a screwdriver
- Ruler
- Scissors
- Pencil
- Stick-on Velcro®
- Stick-on hook

1. Before you start, draw a plan of where you want the items on your organizer to go. Measure the door and cut your wallpaper to size; making it slightly smaller than the door for a neater finish. Paste the door with the glue or Mod Podge® and neatly apply the paper. Smooth out any wrinkles or bubbles before it dries. Once dried, apply another coat of glue or clear varnish to protect it.

2. Measure your white board and clipboard and lightly mark on the door with pencil where they will go. If you have shelves in the cupboard take care not to add any fixings directly in front of them as this may hinder the door closing. Using the sticky Velcro®, attach the white board to the door. Add the sticky hook for the clipboard.

3. Take three bulldog clips, measure and mark on the door where they will go. Using the small screws, attach the clips to the door.

4. Take the card and, using the envelope template as a guide, cut out three envelope pieces. The size depends on how much space you have. Fold in the edges and stitch down to secure, leaving the top open.

5. You can add labels or tapes here to decorate. These will be attached by the three bulldog clips.

6. If you have any room left on the door, add some more bulldog clips using the same method as before.

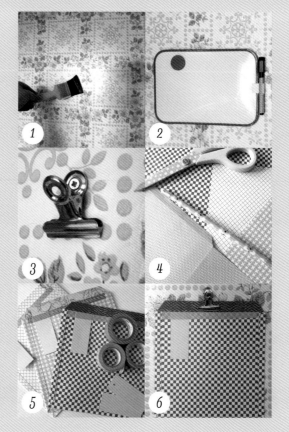

Tips

- This organizer can be adapted to fit any size door. You could have one for each house member or one for school letters and reminders and one for work or bills.

- You can switch the white board for a mini chalkboard or you could paint the whole door with chalkboard paint instead of using the wallpaper.

- The bulldog clips could hold mini message boards or note pads.

- Once a month, sort through everything and get rid of any out-of-date or no-longer-needed bits to keep it tidy and organized.

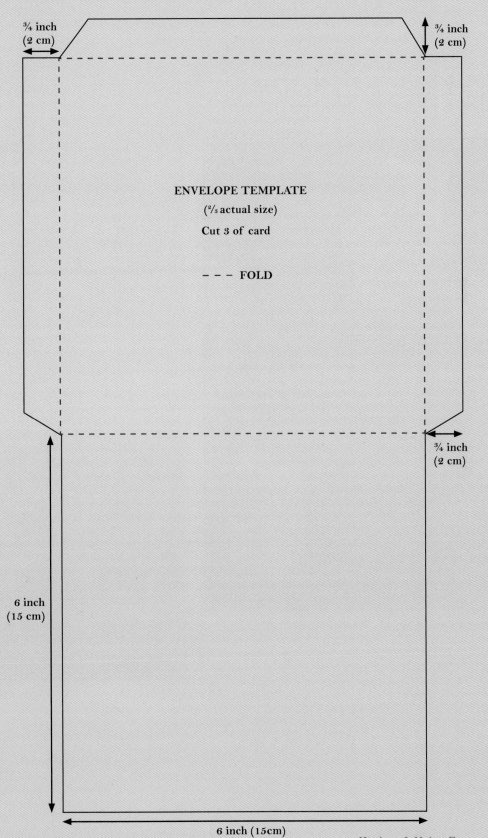

ENVELOPE TEMPLATE

(⅔ actual size)

Cut 3 of card

– – – **FOLD**

¾ inch
(2 cm)

¾ inch
(2 cm)

¾ inch
(2 cm)

6 inch
(15 cm)

6 inch (15cm)

Further Ideas

If you don't have enough wall space in your kitchen for a memo board, you could paint your fridge door with chalkboard paint.

Keep a small jar in the kitchen filled with spare buttons, needles, scissors and threads. This is always handy for emergency repairs and you can easily see the contents.

The vast array of exotic colors present in a herb and spice collection is the perfect excuse for turning it into a display piece. Be inventive with your holder; this old drink bottle crate adds a touch of vintage character.

Tip
Clear out your cupboards often. Not only will you create space, but you will also discover useful items you never knew you had.

Switch your laundry powder boxes for pretty glass jars and keep the washing up equipment all together in vintage bowls.

Chapter 3

LIVING ROOM

Create a relaxing space for yourself using simple storage solutions and clever organization. Cleanse your living space and kick back in the evening without that corner of clutter nagging at you while you watch your favorite movie or entertain guests.

LIVING ROOM

Whatever you use this room for, it's nice to have a tidy and relaxed space in which to kick back and unwind.

Crates or baskets are useful for storing throws or spare cushions, and you can turn crates on their sides to multipurpose as tables. Side tables or trolleys can be useful storage for stationery or gadgets. Use ties to control cables and wires from televisions and media players, and have a place to keep remote controls handy.

Place magazines tidily in neat holders, and after you have read them, recycle or pass them on to make room for new issues.

If you have bookshelves, arranging your books in color order will make them look less cluttered and will brighten up the entire room. Another idea is to make dust jackets from pretty papers to cover the books. If you don't have built-in storage, old cupboards painted-up and given new handles can be handy for storing DVDs, CDs, or photo albums.

Storage Tubs on page 63

Magazine Holders on page 62

Magazine Holders

Stacks of magazines look nicer and are easier to find if they are organized into upright holders and filed into subjects or titles. This project uses medium-sized mailing boxes, wrapping paper and sticky tape. For a neat look, make sure they are all the same height. The metal cardholders are a good way to label them and can be found at scrapbooking or stationery suppliers.

TOOLS & MATERIALS (for 2 boxes)

- 2 medium-size flat-pack mailing boxes. The ones here measure 14½ x 10¼ x 6¼ inch (37 x 26 x 16 cm)
- Scissors
- Craft knife
- Pencil
- Ruler
- Double-sided tape
- Masking tape
- Laundry pegs
- 2 large sheets of good-quality wrapping paper
- 2 metal label holders
- Magazine

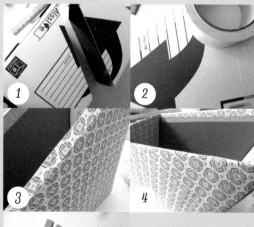

1. Assemble the box as per the instructions. Using a magazine as a guide for the size, draw the design of the holder onto the box. Using the craft knife and ruler, carefully cut along the pencil lines.

2. Put the masking tape along all the edges and corners, to help keep it all in place and secure.

3. To cover the box you will need to cut the papers for the two side panels slightly larger than the box, so the edges will wrap around the corners.

4. Take a sheet of the wrapping paper and place right side facing down. Using the magazine holder as a template, draw around the two sides, adding an extra ⅜ inch (1 cm) all the way around. Then draw around the back, front and base and cut out as it is without the extra ⅜ inch (1 cm). Starting with the two sides, apply the double-sided tape to the paper and stick on to the holder, making sure to smooth out any creases. Fold over the excess paper and press down. Add the double-sided tape to the other pieces and stick on.

5. Place a few laundry pegs along the edges for an hour or so to secure the paper in place, before gluing a label holder to the outside edge.

Storage Tubs

These tubs are handy for any space, but they work well in a living room. You can keep things like TV remotes and small gadgets in them or the larger ones will hold a book or a few magazines. They are reinforced with interfacing so they stand up, and the tops can be rolled down or left as is. The fabrics are all cotton-based so that you can use a hot iron to apply the interfacing. The best fabric I found for these tubs was medium-weight craft cotton with a lighter weight lining.

TOOLS & MATERIALS

For the large tub:

- 1 piece of outer fabric measuring 23¾ x 27½ inch (60 x 70 cm)
- 1 piece of lining fabric measuring 23¾ x 27½ inch (60 x 70 cm)
- 1 piece of heavy-weight iron-on interfacing measuring 23¾ x 27½ inch (60 x 70 cm)

For the medium tub:

- 1 piece of outer fabric measuring 19¾ x 23½ inch (50 x 59.5 cm)
- 1 piece of lining fabric measuring 19¾ x 23½ inch (50 x 59.5 cm)
- 1 piece of heavy-weight iron-on interfacing measuring 19¾ x 23½ inch (50 x 59.5 cm)

For the small tub:

- 1 piece of outer fabric measuring 15¾ x 19¾ inch (40 x 50 cm)

- 1 piece of lining fabric measuring 15¾ x 19¾ inch (40 x 50 cm)
- 1 piece of heavy-weight iron-on interfacing measuring 15¾ x 19¾ inch (40 x 50 cm)
- Sewing machine
- Thread
- Iron—if you have an ironing board, this helps when pressing the tubs but is not essential
- Pins
- Scissors
- Pencil
- Paper
- Ruler
- Drawing compass or circular object to draw around

1. Make a paper pattern for each size tub, using the storage tub templates as a guide and following the measurements opposite. Cut out the fabrics as instructed on the template guide.

2. Take the outer fabric pieces and interfacing. Iron the interfacing onto the wrong side of the fabric.

3. Fold the rectangle in half with right sides together and sew up the side using a ⅜ inch (1 cm) seam to make the tub part. Take the circle and pin to the bottom hem of the tub, right sides together. Because you are sewing a curved edge to a straight edge you will need to sew this together slowly, feeding the fabric gently through. Use a small stitch to give more control.

4. Once the base is sewn, snip carefully into the seam allowance to allow the seams to curve. Turn the right way out and press.

5. Take the lining fabrics and sew together in the same way (minus the interfacing). Leave the lining the wrong way out and place inside the outer tub. Press over a ⅜ inch (1 cm) seam on the top hem of the lining and outer tub, pin and sew together close to the edge.

6. Roll down the top to show the contrast lining.

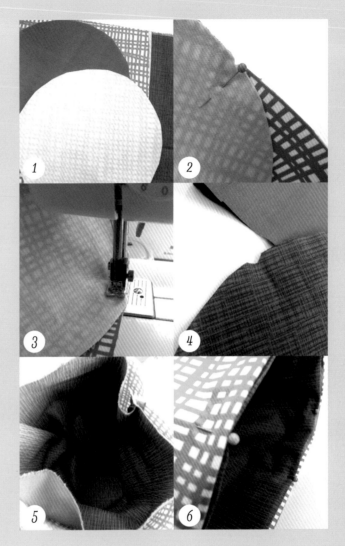

Tips
- These tubs are great for other rooms. You could scale them up to bigger versions and store blankets or cushions in them. Skip the roll-down part and add handles at the top so you can hang them up.

- If you can't find iron-on interfacing you can use the sew-on kind instead.

STORAGE TUB TEMPLATES (⅕ actual size)

Cut 1 of main fabric; Cut 1 of lining fabric; Cut 1 of interfacing of each template

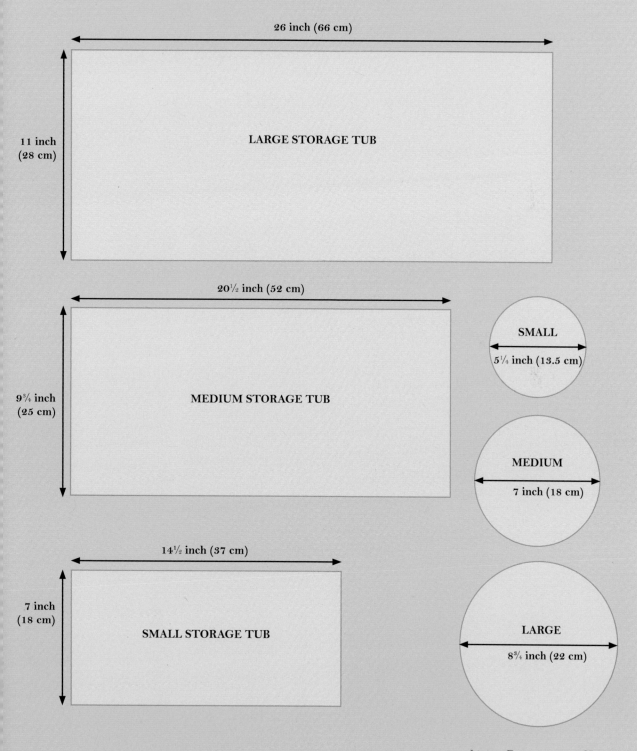

26 inch (66 cm)

11 inch
(28 cm)

LARGE STORAGE TUB

20½ inch (52 cm)

9¾ inch
(25 cm)

MEDIUM STORAGE TUB

SMALL

5¼ inch (13.5 cm)

MEDIUM

7 inch (18 cm)

14½ inch (37 cm)

7 inch
(18 cm)

SMALL STORAGE TUB

LARGE

8¾ inch (22 cm)

Storage Cart

This kind of portable storage is really versatile. The project requires a bar cart or tea trolley, which can often be found in thrift shops or antique stores in a kind of brassy and fake wood state, but you can also pick them up new. The paint used here is a metal paint as it is hard-wearing and will stand up to a few knocks, and the fabric used for the trays is a vinyl oilcloth so it is easy to keep clean.

TOOLS & MATERIALS

- Bar cart or tea trolley with 2 or 3 trays
- Metal paint
- White primer or undercoat
- Paintbrushes

- Masking tape
- 3¼ feet (1 m) vinyl oilcloth fabric
  Note: you may use less depending on how many trays you need to cover.

- Double-sided sticky tape
- Scissors
- Pencil

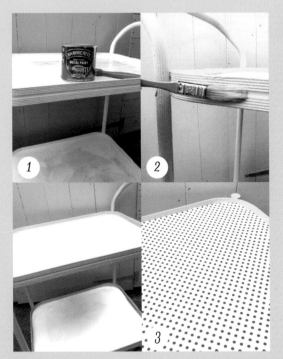

1. Make sure the cart is clean and dry. Mask off any areas you don't want to paint, such as the wheels. In a well-ventilated space, paint a layer of the primer or undercoat and allow to dry thoroughly.

2. Apply the metal paint; several thin coats works better and is more hardwearing than one thick coat. Allow to dry overnight.

3. Take the oilcloth fabric and place over the tray. Using a pencil, trace around the shape of the tray and cut out. Add double-sided tape to the back of the fabric and stick down, smoothing out any creases or air bubbles. Repeat with the other trays.

Tip
- If you can't find a cart you could make one from a small side table by adding casters to the legs, painting it and adding fabric.

Further Ideas

You don't need to throw out old magazines and records if they are valuable to you. They can also look good on display if stored in a suitable container to help keep them tidy.

Tip

Life is too short to hide away your collections and keepsakes, so use your living room as an opportunity to show them off. Use your imagination to find a way of displaying them while at the same time protecting them.

Small spaces can be brightened up with a little color coordination. The key is to keep the amount of colors to a minimum, for a bright yet simple look.

Customize your functional cabinets with pretty paper to brighten them up and conceal the dull contents.

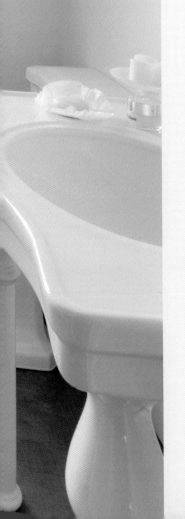

Chapter 4

BATHROOM

Nobody looks forward to picking their way through a messy bathroom, but it doesn't have to be that way if you set up a good routine and a few rules. Simplify the available space by customizing soap bottles and containers, and organizing your storage to keep things sweet, neat, and minimal.

BATHROOM

Storage and organization is vital for a neat and tidy bathroom. Tall, narrow cupboards, such as gym-style lockers, are great as they take up very little floor space and are perfect for keeping towels and toiletries hidden. If you use a shower curtain, keep a spare so you can switch and wash regularly to keep them clean and mold free. Encourage everyone who takes a shower or bath to rinse and clean them afterwards; it only takes a minute.

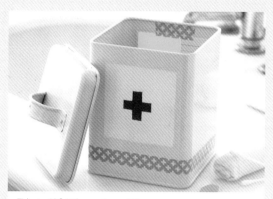

First Aid Tin on page 76

Try to keep the shampoo and soap bottles on show to a minimum, and transfer your usual brands to smaller containers that save room around your shower or bath area. You can customize your own bottles with waterproof labels or tags. If you keep a first aid box in here, make sure it is well stocked and easy to find but in a safe place.

Don't forget the back of the door for extra storage. Even the space above the doorway can be used with a shelf to store toilet rolls or spare towels.

You could consider using small baskets for specific products or house members; they can be stored away and brought out when needed to keep surfaces clear. Pick a regular day or time to clean and tidy the bathroom and check on supplies. Seek out multipurpose, natural

cleaning products to save space on bottles. Keep everything you need to clean the room in a small basket so you can grab it and do a few jobs while waiting for the bath to run.

Have a bathroom wrap or bag ready filled with travel-sized toiletries and a few first aid items for unexpected trips or sleepovers; this saves hunting down spare items and means you don't have to sneak off with the family toothpaste.

When shopping for supplies, choose products with similar packaging or colors for a neater look. Something as simple as dyeing towels the same colors or tones can make a room look neater. Look for mirrors with shelves to double up on wall space.

Towel Roller

Neat piles of soft, fluffy towels in cupboards or draped neatly over towel racks are an ideal scene for your bathroom—although the reality is often a little different. To keep the room tidier in between baths and showers you could try this towel roller idea. It works well because it stays nice and neat up on its hanger until it's ready to be changed for washing. It's simple and takes up very little space. You will need a wooden dowel, small screws, and a leather belt.

TOOLS & MATERIALS

- Wooden dowel ¾ inch (2 cm) diameter and at least 21¼ inch (54 cm) long
- Sandpaper
- Small wood saw
- Masking tape
- Acrylic paint to match the belt color
- Paintbrush
- 1 leather belt
- 2 screws
- Screwdriver
- Scissors
- Pencil
- Ruler or tape measure
- 1 towel measuring at least 15¾ x 43¼ inch (40 x 110 cm) or more if you plan to make a few
- Sewing machine
- Thread
- Iron

To make the holder

1. Using the wood saw, cut the dowel to 21¼ inch (54 cm) long and smooth any rough edges with the sandpaper.

2. Apply some masking tape approximately ¾ inch (2 cm) in from the end of the dowel and repeat at the other end. Paint the ends and allow to dry thoroughly.

To make the straps

3. Cut two pieces from the belt measuring 6¼ inch (16 cm) each, avoiding the bits with the holes and buckles.

To make the towel

4. Cut the towel to measure 15 x 42½ inch (38 x 108 cm).

5. To finish the edges, roll over the hem twice and stitch down. Repeat on the other side. Take the top and bottom of the towel and place together overlapping slightly, right sides facing up.

6. Zigzag stitch along the raw edge to finish. Flip it over and repeat the same stitch on the reverse. You should now have a loop of toweling.

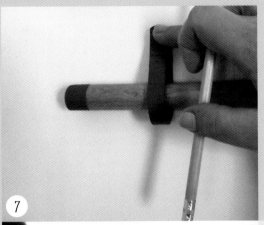

To fix the holder onto the door

7. Place the dowel in the center of the door and measure in 2¼ inch (6 cm) from each end. This is where the leather straps will go. Sit the dowel in the straps and mark the position on the door with a pencil, ensuring the height suits everyone.

8. Using the screws, fix the leather loops to the door. You can remove the dowel while you fix in the screws.

9. To hang the towel, thread the pole through one strap then add the towel and thread through the other strap. Reverse this to remove the towel.

Tips

- This idea is great for a small bathroom or washroom. You could also make one for a kitchen and fix it to the side of the work counter.

- Toweling is pretty hard to find in nice patterns, but you could use a good-quality heavier weight cotton fabric too.

- If you prefer a natural look, paint the ends of the pole white and use a tan or brown belt instead.

First Aid Tin

Most households have a first aid box or bag somewhere. It's a good idea to keep an edited version in the bathroom to save trips downstairs in the middle of the night for headache medication or calamine lotion. This project uses a tea-caddy type tin because it is a handy size and shape for a high cupboard and tall enough for medicine bottles.

TOOLS & MATERIALS

- A tea caddy or tin with a lid
- Spray paint in white and pink or red
- Masking tape
- Card
- Scissors or craft knife
- Washi tapes for decorating

1. If your tin has a print or words on it, you will want to cover this. Mask off a square shape on the front of the tin and apply a thin coat of the white spray paint into the square. Follow the paint instructions carefully and do the spraying outside in a well-ventilated space. Allow to dry, then apply a second coat.

2. Carefully cut out a cross shape stencil in the card using the craft knife. When the white paint is dry, place the stencil in the center of the white square, using masking tape to keep it in position. With your red or pink spray paint, fill inside the cross stencil.

3. Leave to dry. Add a line of washi tape along the bottom of the tin for decoration.

4. Gather your supplies, checking that they haven't expired, and add an easy-to-find contact list to your tin with emergency phone numbers.

Tips

- This first aid tin could be graded up to a full-sized version using a larger cookie tin. You could spray paint the tin all one color and then follow the DIY opposite for the label. Scale it right down to a handy portable version using a small travel-sized candy tin or plastic box.

- If you don't have spray paint you can use enamel-type paint and a brush instead.

- A good tip is to buy a few smaller travel-sized versions of medicines and lotions so they fit neatly inside. This also means you will have spares handy for holidays or trips.

Bathroom Wrap

This portable wrap is ideal for keeping travel-sized toiletries and sleepover essentials handy. Inside there are five pockets for storage and it will roll up neatly so it doesn't take up too much room in your travel bag or bathroom cupboard. You won't need a lot of fabric for this, just a few fat quarters of craft cottons, a length of quilt batting and whatever trims you have on hand. The small travel-size bottles that you find in the holiday section of supermarkets are perfect for this. Add some small first aid items to keep it well stocked, so you can just throw it in your overnight bag when you need it.

TOOLS & MATERIALS

- A piece of fabric for the outer cover measuring 15¾ x 11¾ inch (40 x 29.5 cm)
- A piece of fabric for the inner cover measuring 15¾ x 11¾ inch (40 x 29.5 cm)
- A piece of fabric for the pockets measuring 15¾ x 11¾ inch (40 x 29.5 cm)
- 15¾ inch (40 cm) of ric-rac trim
- 39½ inch (1 m) of bias binding
- Quilt batting measuring 15¾ x 11¾ inch (40 x 29.5 cm)

- Sewing machine
- Paper
- Ruler
- Pencil
- Iron
- Scissors
- Pins
- Thread

1. Using the bathroom wrap template as a guide, draw on to paper and cut out a rectangle measuring 15 x 9¾ inch (38 cm x 25 cm) for the outer and inner cover.

2. On another piece of paper draw a rectangle 15 x 6¾ inch (38 x 17 cm) for the pocket template. Following the guide on the templates cut out your pieces in fabric.

Tips

- This roll can be made to any size, so you can scale it up for larger bottles or brushes. Use a waterproof material so it will wipe clean.

- If you don't have quilt batting you can use fleece or just add an extra layer of thick fabric inside.

- This wrap would also work as a cosmetic brush holder or craft wrap for holding crochet hooks or sewing supplies.

To make the pockets

3. Lay your pocket fabric out and fold in half. Take 15¾ inch (40 cm) of your binding, fold in half and stitch it onto the folded edge of your pocket fabric. Take the ric-rac trim and position it 2¼ inch (6 cm) below the binding and stitch into place. Press, and put this pocket piece to one side for now.

4. Take the inner cover fabric and pin to the batting with right sides facing up. Stitch some diagonal, crisscross quilting lines across the whole piece.

5. Take your quilted inner cover and place the pocket piece on top, right sides facing upward, and pin together. Measure and mark where your pocket stitch lines will go; the ones shown here are approximately 2¾ inch (7 cm) apart, but you can adjust these if you need to. Starting at the top, neatly stitch down the lines to create the pockets.

To make the ties

6. Using the remaining piece of binding, fold over and stitch down to create a narrow strip. Fold in half and pin on the right side halfway down. These will be attached later when you sew everything together. Make sure the open ends of the binding are facing inward.

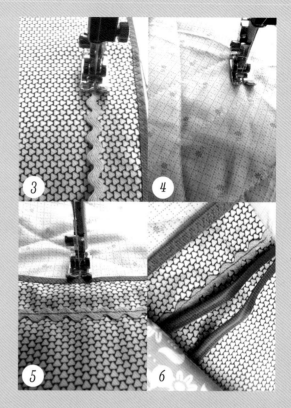

Sewing together

7. Take your outer fabric and place on top of the quilted and pocket pieces right sides together.

8. Pin around the edges and sew together with a ⅜ inch (1 cm) seam, and backstitch over the part where the ties are attached for added strength. Leave a gap of 4 inch (10 cm) for turning out.

9. Trim the seams and corners and turn the right way round. Press the seams flat. To close up the opening, topstitch neatly all the way around, close to the edge.

BATHROOM WRAP TEMPLATES (⅓ actual size)

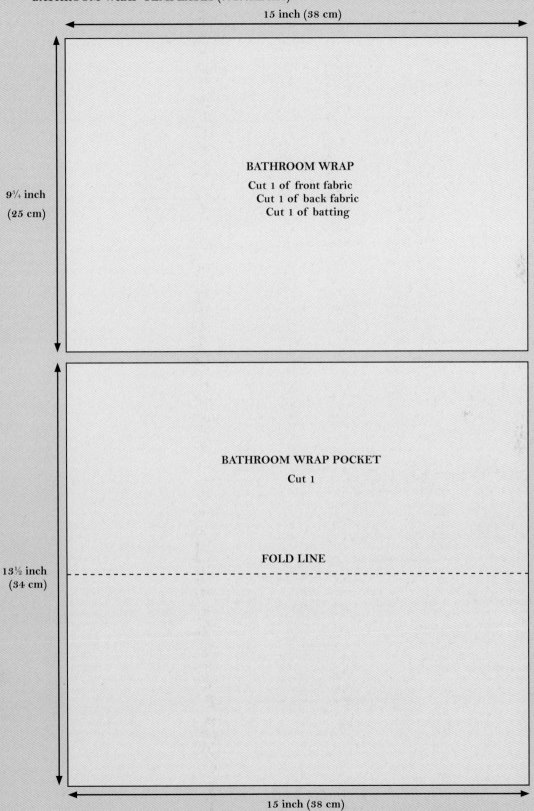

15 inch (38 cm)

9¾ inch
(25 cm)

BATHROOM WRAP

Cut 1 of front fabric
Cut 1 of back fabric
Cut 1 of batting

BATHROOM WRAP POCKET

Cut 1

FOLD LINE

13½ inch
(34 cm)

15 inch (38 cm)

Further Ideas

Makeshift curtains will hide all your cleaning products and brighten up your bathroom.

Tip
Be realistic about what you use. The space occupied by old containers will be invaluable.

Give each member of the family their own container and attach them to walls to keep them out of the way.

Cotton swabs   Brushes   Tissues

These tins will help you locate essential items easily.

Suspending from walls will create more surface space as well as enabling you to easily reach what you need.

Chapter 5

BEDROOM

Sleep comes easily in a calm, relaxing space. Take the time to keep your bedroom clear of junk and laundry, and organize your storage so you can put things away easily and find things quickly. And if you make your bed, you are less likely to climb straight back into it.

BEDROOM

Keeping this room tidy is a big time saver, and your sleep won't be disturbed by toppling piles of clothes or junk. It's tempting to put things in your bedroom that are waiting to find a home, but unless you move them on pretty quickly they tend to accumulate and take root!

Hidden storage is a good start. Try to pick the largest furniture your room and budget will allow. Utilize spaces on top of wardrobes with boxes or baskets, and use similar colors or textures to keep the room from looking too busy. Try to find bedside stands with cupboards or drawers to maximize storage. Blanket boxes or trunks are great for storing spare throws and quilts and can be turned into a seat by placing cushions on top. Keep bedding together by folding items neatly together and placing the whole set inside one of the pillowcases.

Organize your drawers with internal compartments for smaller items; you can buy these but you could make your own from small cardboard boxes. If you have space under your bed a couple of nice vintage suitcases can keep the clutter in order. Label the cases so you know what's inside.

For discreet jewelry storage, add a few hooks to the inside of the wardrobe door and hang necklaces from them. Look out for pretty bowls and tins to keep smaller things like earrings and barrettes in. Keep the closet floor clear for shoe storage. Collect shoeboxes and cover them in

Luggage Tags on page 87

pretty fabrics and papers, filling them with less used shoes and labeling the boxes. Hang tall boots on padded trouser hangers to keep their shape. Use narrow hangers so they take up less space and arrange your wardrobe in styles or color. Sort through your clothes every few months to see if there are things you could pass on or recycle.

Store out-of-season clothing in garment bags and use lavender bags to keep the moths away.

Luggage Tags

These labels are inspired by old-fashioned luggage tags, which gives them a vintage look. You can use them for labeling stored clothes in suitcases, baskets on high, hard-to-reach shelves, or anything that is to be stored away.

TOOLS & MATERIALS

- 5 felt pieces in your chosen colors, minimum size 4¾ x 7¾ inch (11.5 x 20 cm)
- Medium-weight sew-on interfacing
- Card
- Sharpie pen or stickers for labeling
- Clear plastic sheet— I re-used the packaging that came with some bedding
- Sewing machine
- Pins
- Contrast thread
- Pencil
- Paper
- 19¾ inch (50 cm) of bias binding
- 5 narrow belts ⅝ inch (1.5 cm) wide with buckle
- Scissors
- Ruler
- Bradawl or small screwdriver to make holes in the belts

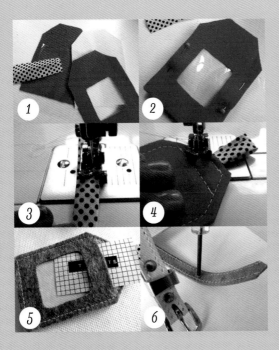

1. Make a paper template of the tag using the luggage tag template on page 88 as a guide. Cut out all the materials as instructed.

2. Cut out the opening and the window square on the front piece. Sandwich the pieces together in this order: back felt piece, interfacing, plastic, front felt piece, and pin together.

3. Take the binding and fold in half width-ways, stitch together, fold in half and place the open ends of the binding in between the layers to form a loop.

4. Using a contrast thread, begin sewing the layers together; backstitch where the binding loop is attached to secure.

5. Cut out a piece of card to fit inside the window and add your words using stickers or pen. Insert the card into the tag.

6. Cut the belts to 9½ inch (24 cm) in length. Using the bradawl, make a new hole for the buckle. Thread the belt through the binding loop to attach to the tag.

LUGGAGE TAG TEMPLATE

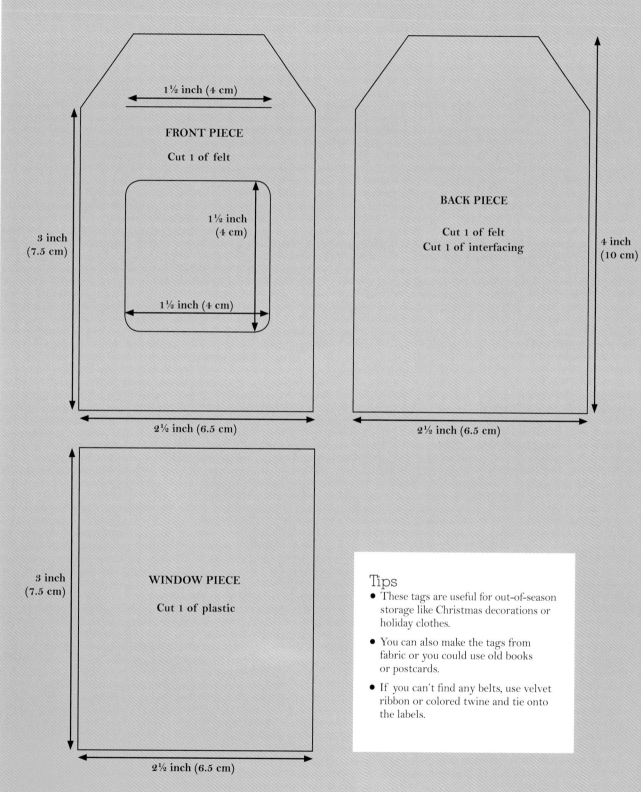

FRONT PIECE

Cut 1 of felt

1½ inch (4 cm)

1½ inch (4 cm)

1½ inch (4 cm)

3 inch (7.5 cm)

2½ inch (6.5 cm)

BACK PIECE

Cut 1 of felt
Cut 1 of interfacing

4 inch (10 cm)

2½ inch (6.5 cm)

WINDOW PIECE

Cut 1 of plastic

3 inch (7.5 cm)

2½ inch (6.5 cm)

Tips
- These tags are useful for out-of-season storage like Christmas decorations or holiday clothes.
- You can also make the tags from fabric or you could use old books or postcards.
- If you can't find any belts, use velvet ribbon or colored twine and tie onto the labels.

Garment Bags

These garment bags are made from vintage fabrics and look pretty hanging together on a rail. They are great for storing out-of-season clothes or special occasion outfits as they keep the garments clean and dust free. The pockets are handy for storing any accessories or spare buttons. You can choose the length depending on the garments to be stored in them—dresses and coats will need longer bags—or you can leave the hem open so any length will fit.

TOOLS & MATERIALS (for one medium-length garment bag)

- A piece of fabric measuring 47¼ x 39½ inch (1.2 x 1 m)
- A 27½ inch (70 cm) length of bias binding
- Fabric scraps and trims for pockets
- Coat hanger
- A large piece of paper; wallpaper is good for this

- Pencil
- Scissors
- Thread
- Sewing machine
- Iron

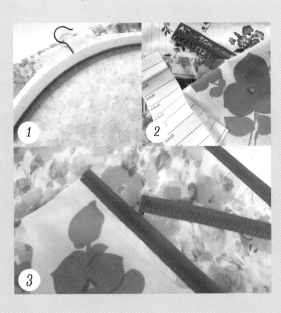

1. Draft a paper pattern by laying the paper on a flat surface and placing the hanger at the top. Using the garment bag template on page 91 as a guide, draw the outline of the garment bag, making sure the pattern is at least 2 inch (5 cm) wider at each side than the hanger width. For the length, measure a garment you will be keeping in the bag. Add an extra ⅜ inch (1 cm) all the way around for the seam allowance. Cut around the shape.

2. Using the paper pattern, cut out two identical fabric pieces. Cut out a rectangle of a contrasting fabric for the pocket and any trims you would like to add.

Binding the neck edges

3. Take the top neck edge of one piece and attach the folded contrast bias binding by straight stitching along the edge, making sure to catch the binding on both sides. Repeat with the other piece.

To make the pocket

4. Take another length of the binding and fold over the top edge of the pocket piece. Stitch down as before. Fold over the edges of the other three sides and press flat. Fold over again and sew a running stitch around all four sides. Press again and pin into place at the center of the front piece. Add any trims. Attach the pocket by sewing down three sides, leaving the top bound edge open.

Sewing up the bags

5. With the right sides facing each other, pin the two main pieces together down each side and sew together using a ⅜ inch (1 cm) seam allowance, leaving the hem open. You can zigzag stitch or serge the raw seam edges for a neater finish. Fold over the hem twice and press, pin in place and stitch down. Turn the right way round and press.

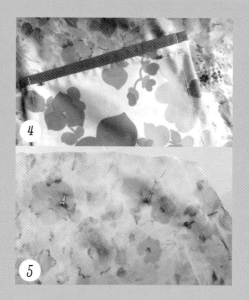

Tips

- There are several variations of this garment bag you could try; if you have some smaller fabric pieces you could patch them together or use different fabrics for the back and front.

- You can also make dust covers for just the top of your garments by making extra short versions using pillowcases.

- You can add Velcro® or buttons at the hem to keep it closed and add a ribbon loop at the bottom so the garment bag can be folded in half and hooked over the hanger for transporting, however don't use Velcro® if you are storing knitted or delicate garments in it.

- You could move the pocket to the inside and keep a scented dryer sheet or lavender bags in it to keep the clothes smelling nice.

- Switch the floral prints for checks or stripes and they would make good suit bags.

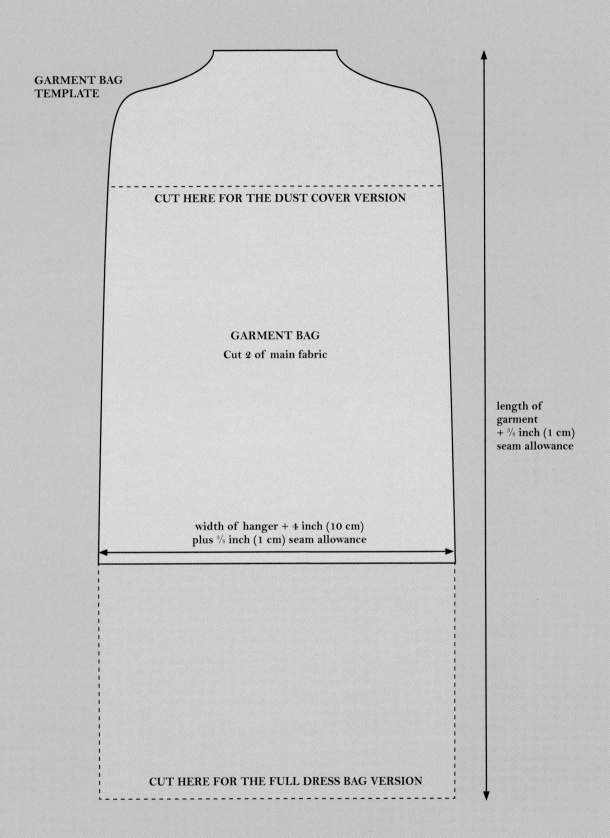

**GARMENT BAG
TEMPLATE**

CUT HERE FOR THE DUST COVER VERSION

GARMENT BAG

Cut 2 of main fabric

length of
garment
+ ⅜ inch (1 cm)
seam allowance

width of hanger + 4 inch (10 cm)
plus ⅜ inch (1 cm) seam allowance

CUT HERE FOR THE FULL DRESS BAG VERSION

Gadget Case

This pretty case is perfect for keeping your tech handy by your bedside. The front pocket has been added to provide a home for headphones or charging cables. It will keep your gadget safe and your nightstand tidy. Pick fabrics that will look good in your bedroom. The sizing depends on what you will be using it for; the case shown here is for a standard size iPad. The fabric is a light to medium weight and is lined with polyester fleece for a soft, padded feel.

TOOLS & MATERIALS (for a regular size iPad tablet)

- Fabric measuring 19¾ inch (50 cm) square
- Polyester fleece measuring 13¾ x 19¾ inch (35 x 50 cm)
- 9¾ inch (25 cm) length of ric-rac trim
- 4 inch (10 cm) length of narrow cord or ribbon
- 1 button
- Scissors

- Pencil
- Paper
- Pins
- Measuring tape
- Sewing machine
- Thread
- Hand sewing needle

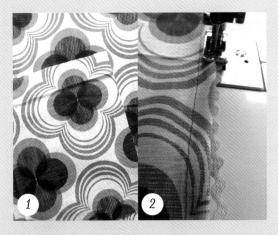

To make the pocket

1. Measure your gadget. Whatever the size, you need to make the case big enough for it to fit comfortably inside so add an extra 1 inch (2.5 cm) to each side and the top and bottom to also accommodate the seam allowance. Following these measurements and the gadget case template on page 95 as a guide, make a paper pattern of the main piece and pocket piece. Use the paper pattern to cut out the fabric and fleece.

2. Take the front pocket piece and fold over the top hem twice and stitch down. Add the ric-rac trim to the reverse side of the pocket so just the scallop edges are visible and carefully sew on.

Sewing the pocket and case together

3. Lay down one of the main fabric pieces with right side facing up, and place the pocket piece right side also facing upward on top, making sure the sides and bottom hem match up. Take the other main fabric piece and place on top with right side facing down. The pocket should be sandwiched in between. Pin together. Using a ⅜ inch (1 cm) seam allowance, sew around the sides and base, leaving the top edge open. Trim the seams. Turn the case the right way out and press.

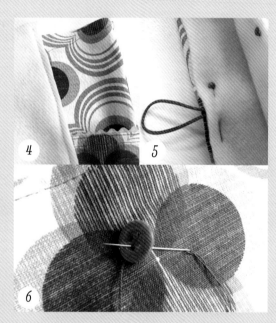

Sewing the fleece inner

4. Take the two pieces of fleece and put right sides together; this is not always obvious with fleece so just make sure they both look the same. Using a ⅜ inch (1 cm) seam allowance, sew around the sides and base leaving the top edge open.

Sewing together and finishing

5. Leave the fleece liner inside out and place inside the outer case. Fold over and press the top edges of both pieces inward and pin together. Measure the center point of the back opening and add the loop of cord, tucking the ends well into the lining. Pin securely in place.

6. Stitch down around the top, close to the edge. Make sure to backstitch over the loop to secure. Press. Mark where the button will go and securely sew it into position.

Tips

- This case is also handy for travel as it will keep your gadgets clean and protected.

- For a different version you could try making the outer case in oilcloth or waterproof fabric.

- If you want to simplify the project you can switch the fabric for a thick felt and just make the same way but without the lining.

- You can also make mini versions in the same way for phones or iPods or bigger versions for laptops.

- If you want to add more pockets, just make the back in the same way as the front.

GADGET CASE TEMPLATES

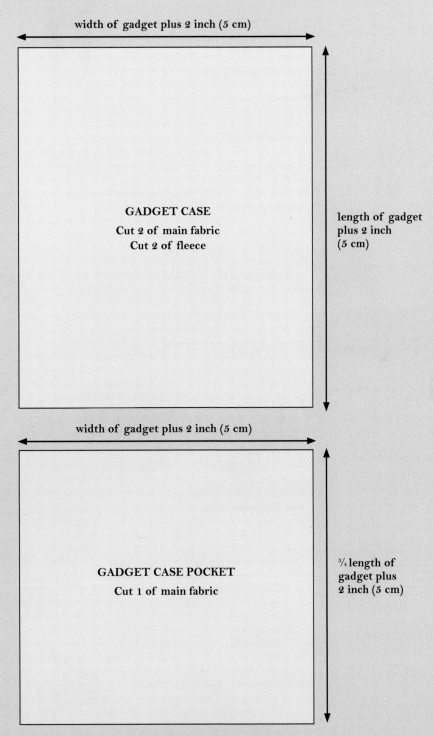

width of gadget plus 2 inch (5 cm)

GADGET CASE
Cut 2 of main fabric
Cut 2 of fleece

length of gadget
plus 2 inch
(5 cm)

width of gadget plus 2 inch (5 cm)

GADGET CASE POCKET
Cut 1 of main fabric

$\frac{3}{4}$ length of
gadget plus
2 inch (5 cm)

Further Ideas

A wardrobe containing different compartments will help you easily identify items of clothing.

Tip

Regular clear-outs will keep clutter to a minimum. Turn them into a fun event such as a clothes swap evening or yard sale.

Raid your kitchen for small, pretty containers you can store your jewelry in.

Tip

Keeping your trinkets and jewelry visible will ensure you actually wear them, especially when you're getting ready in a hurry.

Place folded bed covers and sheets inside a pillowcase to keep sets neat and organized.

Chapter 6

KIDS' ROOM

You need to maximize the space you have here and make tidying away a game rather than a chore. Create storage solutions that look great and work to keep the floors clear (and bedtime easier). Be inventive with colors, funky shapes and labels by unleashing your inner child and having some fun.

KIDS' ROOM

Pajama Case on page 108

This room may double-up as a playroom, so if you keep games and toys in here they will need good storage for hiding away at nighttime to prevent distractions. Under-bed boxes with wheels are useful, or peg rails with bags for small items look cute. There are lots of plastic boxes out there to put toys in, but an old picnic basket or a soft suitcase would work just as well. Painted metal pails look great filled with brightly colored toys. Try spray painting some and stenciling words or letters on them.

For books you could add some legs to an old drawer, stack the books inside with the fronts facing so children can see the covers, and rotate them regularly so you don't all get bored of the same stories. Small spice shelves can be added to the side of wardrobes or drawers to hold favorite bedtime books.

If the closet has space, add boxes to the floor for storing out-of-season clothing. You can add an extra rail lower down to double up on hanging space. Labels on drawers can be helpful if you are hoping the kids will put their own clothes away. Storage pockets are good for keeping by the bed, or hang them on the back of doors or in wardrobes for extra space.

Playrooms may be a whole room or sometimes part of the kitchen or living room; either way you will want to see the floor sometimes and be able to walk across it without stepping on little bits and pieces. Children can be overwhelmed with too many play choices, so try keeping most toys stored away and only bring out a small selection each day. Boxes on wheels are good as small children can move these themselves. Low and easy-to-open storage is great for this type of room, as are coat pegs and hooks. It's also nice to have some toys on display and a small shelf holding special treasures is ideal for this.

Check all the toys regularly to thin out any broken or out-grown items. When buying furniture for this space, source multifunctional pieces like storage cubes that can double up as somewhere to sit or benches with lift-up seats. A row of matching baskets with bags inside can look neat and hide away toys at the end of the day. A low table is great for playing games on and crafting. Keep crayons and pens in recycled cans or pails on a high shelf so no extracurricular scribbling occurs on the walls. Buy small boxes to store craft supplies and label them so the contents are easy to find, as well as easily tidied away after use. If books get torn or ruined, don't throw them away; save any favorite pictures and frame them to hang on the wall, or use them to make the labels and tags.

Pegged Pots

These are perfect for storing toys or craft supplies. They can be customized with stencils and stickers, and held in place with bulldog clips.

TOOLS & MATERIALS

- Metal cans or pots. These can be bought new or, even better, recycled
- Strong cord or wire
- Medium-sized bulldog clips

1. Prepare your pots by cleaning and painting them to match the colors of the room they will go in.

2. Stretch the cord so it is fairly taut and suspend it across a wall using hooks or screws at either end.

3. Attach the pots using bulldog clips and make sure the contents don't weigh them down too much.

Tip
- These pots are useful in other rooms too; use them in the kitchen or workrooms.

Magnet Board

This board is a sweet way to display memos or postcards, recipes or inspirational pictures. It is made from a lightweight metal baking sheet and some small wooden discs. You can have great fun making the little magnets look like people you know or members of the family. Wooden discs can be found in craft shops and also come in different shapes and sizes, but circles are perfect for faces or letters. The magnetic strips can also be found in craft shops or hardware stores and should be self-adhesive with a strong, peel-off paper backing.

TOOLS & MATERIALS

- Metal baking sheet
- White paint
- Sticky-back plastic
- Wooden discs in various sizes
- Magnetic strips
- Acrylic or craft paints
- Paintbrush
- Toothpick
- Pencil
- Scissors
- Clear varnish spray
- Sticky Velcro® dots for attaching to the wall

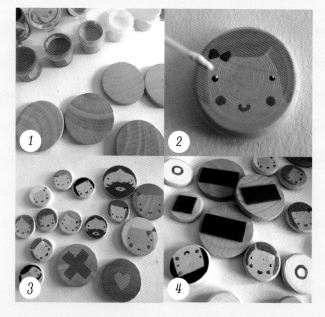

To make the magnets

1. Take the wooden discs and lightly draw the design on with pencil. You can skip this part and just paint straight onto the wood if you like. Carefully start painting, allowing each color to dry to avoid smudging.

2. Use the end of a toothpick to paint on the finer details such as facial features.

3. When you are finished painting the discs, set them down outside and spray with a quick coat of clear varnish to seal.

4. When they are fully dry, turn them over, cut and stick down the magnetic strips onto the back.

To make the magnetic board

5. Make sure the baking sheet is clean and dry. With the right side facing upward, paint the edges of the sheet. You don't need to paint all of it as the sticky-back plastic will cover the main part. When the paint is dry, flip the sheet over and paint all of the back. You may need a couple of coats to cover thoroughly. Allow to dry.

6. Place the sticky-back plastic over the sheet and draw around it. Cut out this shape and peel off the backing to stick down onto the sheet. A good tip here is to start at one corner and slowly peel and press as you go, smoothing out any bubbles or creases. Add magnets.

7. Attach the Velcro® dots to the back of the sheet so it can easily be fixed to a wall or surface.

Tips

- This project can be made out of other metal objects like a tray or plate. If you want to leave out the sticky-back plastic you can just paint the whole thing in a bright color or you could stick fabric or paper on instead, making sure you use extra strong magnetic tape as the fabric can make it harder for the magnets to stick.

- If you don't want to use faces on the magnets, try words or flowers. You could use square pieces and make them into little houses, or geometric shapes would look good just painted as they are.

Toy Shelf

This project is perfect as a wall display for small toys or keepsakes, and the narrow shelves mean they don't take up too much room in a small space. This type of shelf can often be found gathering dust in the back of a thrift store. They vary in shape and style, but for this project you will need a wooden one with a solid back panel. The back is covered with fabric and images from a favorite childhood book, and the added hooks mean it will also provide extra hanging storage.

TOOLS & MATERIALS

- A small wooden spice rack shelf to mount on a wall
- Sandpaper
- Paint
- Paintbrushes
- Scissors

- Paper or fabric for covering the back of the shelf; I have used a combination of fabric and vintage children's book illustrations.
- Mod Podge® or PVA glue

- Newspaper
- 3 medium-sized plastic-coated cup hooks
- Pencil
- Ruler

1. Prepare the shelf by making sure it is clean and dry, and lightly sand the surface to give the wood a rougher finish for applying the paint. Paint all visible parts of the shelf with your chosen color and allow to dry. Allow two or three coats for an even finish. At this point I turned the shelf upside down as I wanted to add hooks to the bottom shelf.

2. Using the newspaper, make a paper template of the back panel for each shelf. Using the template, cut out panels of your fabric and papers. Cutting the panels slightly smaller than you need makes for a neater finish.

3. With the Mod Podge® or PVA glue, stick the panels into place, smoothing out any bubbles or creases as you go. When dry you can apply another coat of PVA or Mod Podge® over the top to give a protective finish.

4. Once the adhesive has dried you can add the hooks to the underside of the lower shelf.

Tips

- This shelf could work in any space or room; it's just the right size for small toys, washi tapes, nail polish, little jars of haberdashery and little ornaments.

- You could switch the book illustrations for graphic comic images or geometric patterns for a teenager's bedroom.

- Paint the whole shelf in a bright, bold color if your room needs brightening up.

Toy Cart

This crate pull-along is just the right size for keeping toys or books in. Although it can be hard to find original apple crates these days, there are reproduction crates widely available that would work just as well. The casters and industrial handles can be found in hardware stores or online. The sides are decorated with old children's book illustrations and the inside is painted with a pop of bright color.

TOOLS & MATERIALS

- A large apple crate
- Sandpaper
- White paint
- Paintbrushes
- Bright colored paint for the inside; a small sample pot will be enough
- Old books; look for old, torn ones in thrift stores so you don't feel as bad cutting them up!
- Mod Podge® or PVA glue
- Clear varnish
- Scissors
- Ruler
- Pencil
- Paper
- 4 casters
- 2 drop latch handles

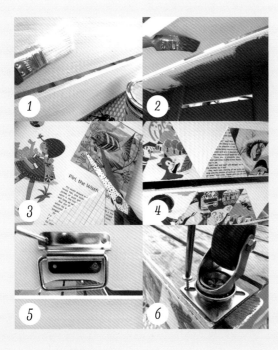

1. Begin by cleaning and sanding the crate to make sure it's ready for painting. Paint the outside of the crate in white. You may need a couple of coats.

2. Paint the inside in the bright color and leave to dry.

3. While the paint is drying, make a triangle template out of paper. Choose images from the book that will look good; try to get a mix of color and maybe a bit of text. Cut the images into triangles. How many you need will depend on the size of your crate, but you can space them out a bit.

4. Using the Mod Podge® or PVA glue, stick the triangles onto the side of the crate.

5. When the glue is dry, add a coat of varnish to the whole thing inside and out to protect it from knocks and scuffs. Attach the handles to each end with screws.

6. Fix the casters to each corner of the base.

Tips

- If you have trouble finding a crate then you could try using a wooden planter or ready-made toy box. You can use a large basket but just add a piece of wood to the base so you can fix the wheels on.

- If you don't have any handles, try drilling a couple of holes in the crate and threading some rope through, then knot at the back.

- This project would work in a craft room for yarn or fabric storage, swapping the book images for vintage dress patterns or knitting patterns.

Pajama Case

Keeping beds tidy in a child's room can be tricky. Sleepwear has a habit of ending up on the floor or crumpled up inside the bedding. This cute face is a secret hiding place for PJs or nightgowns. It is lightly quilted so will hold its shape when empty. The design is easy to adapt for a boy or girl and you can choose the hairstyle and colors to match the owner or the bedroom. Ideally this would be washable, so try to pick easy-care fabrics if possible.

TOOLS & MATERIALS

- Base color fabric for the front and back of the case measuring 47¼ x 19¾ inch (120 x 50 cm)
- Remnants of fabric for hair
- Double-sided fusible interfacing measuring 19¾ inch (50 cm) square
- Fleece or quilt batting measuring 19¾ inch (50 cm) square
- Pink felt
- Embroidery thread in black, orange and pink

- Sewing machine
- Hand-sewing needle
- Iron
- Thread
- Scissors
- Paper
- Pencil
- Large button or flower
- Disappearing marker

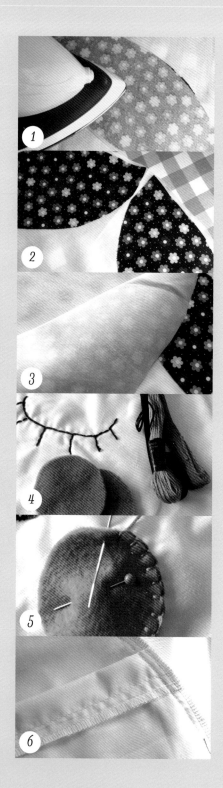

Find a circular object to draw around that is roughly 19¾ inch (50 cm) in diameter. Using the paper, draw around the circle and cut out; this is your paper pattern. Using the pattern as a guide, cut out the template for the back pieces. Sketch out the shape of the hair onto another piece of paper. Cut out one front piece in the base fabric and one in the batting. Cut out two back pieces and the hair fabric pieces.

To make the face

1. Take the fusible interfacing and cut out two pieces in the shape of the hair. Using a hot iron and no steam, fuse the interfacing onto the hair pieces.

2. Peel off the backing paper, position onto the face and fuse into place.

3. Take the batting and pin onto the wrong side of the face.

4. Using the disappearing marker, draw on the eyes and mouth. Hand-stitch the eyes and mouth using the embroidery thread.

5. For the cheeks, cut out two small circles in the pink felt and stitch on.

To make the back

6. Take the two back pieces, fold over the straight edge twice, press flat and stitch down. Lay the pieces on top of the face, right sides together (they should overlap in the center); this will be the opening. Carefully pin the front and back together and, using a ⅜ inch (1 cm) seam, sew around the edge of the circle. You can zigzag or crimp the raw edges with pinking shears to give a neater finish and prevent fraying. Turn the whole thing the right way round and press. Add the button or flower to the hair.

Tips

- There are lots of other ways you could make this case, like adapting it to be an animal using furry fabric, or you could use a heavily patterned design or patchwork and leave the face off.

- If you don't have batting you could switch this for fleece or plain heavy cotton.

- You could use buttons for eyes or draw on the features using a fabric marker pen or fabric paint.

PJ CASE TEMPLATES (⅕ actual size)

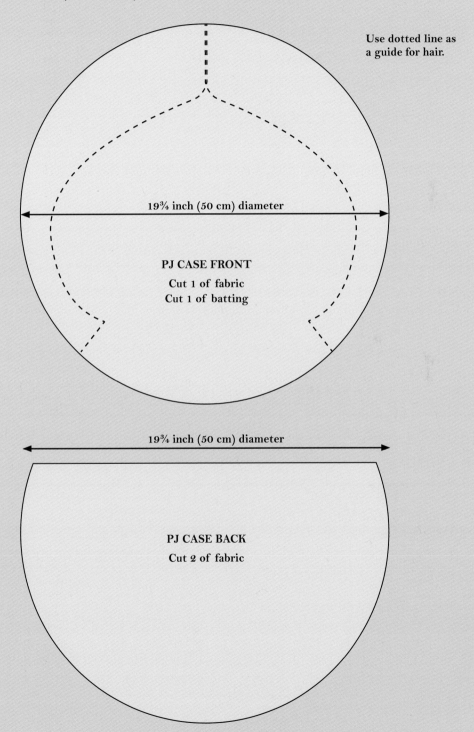

Use dotted line as
a guide for hair.

19¾ inch (50 cm) diameter

PJ CASE FRONT
Cut 1 of fabric
Cut 1 of batting

19¾ inch (50 cm) diameter

PJ CASE BACK
Cut 2 of fabric

Wall Pocket Organizer

This wall pocket is great for kids' rooms as you can hang it on a wall near the bed so they can keep their books and toys handy. It also works well for older children who might want to keep gadgets and technology close by. In a nursery you could keep it by the changing table filled with spare diapers and baby items. The fabrics used here are craft cottons, but you could use heavier weight materials or even recycle some pillowcases or bedding. The pocket hanger is quilted to make it stronger and all the pockets are faced. You will need a couple of wall hooks to hang this. It is pretty sturdy, but to be safe make sure you don't put anything too heavy in the pockets.

TOOLS & MATERIALS

- Patterned fabric measuring 39¼ x 23¾ inch (1 m x 60 cm)
- Plain white fabric measuring 39¼ inch (1 m) square
- Quilt batting measuring 39¼ x 23¾ inch (1 m x 60 cm)
- 6½ feet (2 m) of ¾ inch (2 cm) wide bias binding
- 5 smaller pieces of patterned fabric in the sizes given on page 117

- Scissors
- Pencil
- Ruler or measuring tape
- Sewing machine
- Matching threads
- Pins or safety pins
- Iron

To make the main quilted piece

1. On a large surface, gather your chosen fabric for the front, the quilt batting, and the plain white fabric.

2. Cut a rectangle measuring 37¾ x 21¼ inch (96 x 54 cm) from each piece, using the wall pocket template on page 116. Press the fabrics and sandwich them together by placing the white piece right side facing down, the quilt batting on top, and then the front fabric on top, right side facing up.

3. Smooth out any creases to make sure all three fabrics are nice and flat, and pin them together, keeping the pins away from your stitch line.

4. Quilt the pieces together by carefully stitching rows approximately 6 inch (15 cm) apart going down and across. Trim all around the edges to make sure you have a neat finish. Take the bias binding and cut two pieces 4¾ inch (11.5 cm) in length. Fold these in half width-ways and stitch down to form the hanging loops.

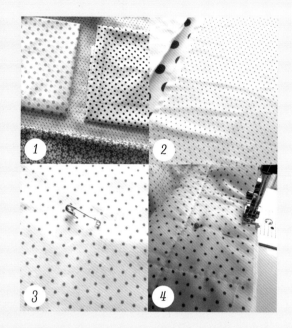

Sewing on the binding

There are so many ways of doing this. This is a machine-stitched method that I use for quilts:

5. Take your bias binding and fold over the end at a 45-degree angle.

6. Place the raw edge of the binding against the edge of the quilted piece with right sides together.

7. Begin sewing 1¼ inch (3 cm) in from the start of the binding and sew ¼ inch (0.6 cm) away from the edge, all the way around. When you get to a corner, stop just before the edge, backstitch to secure and turn the piece 45 degrees. Lift up the binding and then fold back down and begin sewing as before. Repeat the fold at each corner.

8. When you get all the way round, trim away any extra binding. Sew right up to the point where you started.

9. Turn the piece over so that the reverse side is facing upward, fold over the binding and stitch down.

10. Sew inside the original stitch line so the front will look neat, and continue all the way around. Add the two loops to the top and backstitch to secure.

To make the pockets

11. Cut five pieces of fabric using the pocket templates on page 117. Using the white fabric, cut the same size pieces again.

12. Take the pocket pieces and place right side facing up. Lay the white fabric pieces on top with right side facing down. Pin and sew each pocket piece together using a ⅜ inch (1 cm) seam. Don't sew all the way round, and leave an opening of 3¼ inch (8 cm).

13. Trim the corners and turn the pockets the right way round. Press and fold in the opening. Topstitch the pockets. Position the pockets in place on the quilted piece.

14. Make sure they are even and straight. Pin in place and carefully sew down. The larger pocket can be divided into two by stitching a straight line down the center of the pocket.

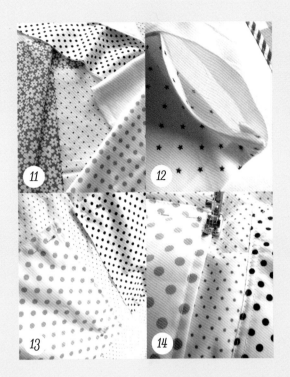

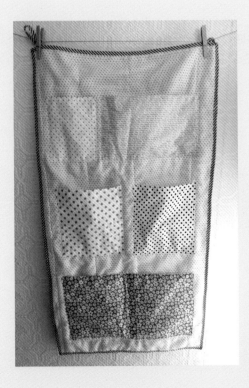

Tips

- This pocket hanger can be adapted to any size or shape. You can make it small enough to hang on the inside of a wardrobe door to store accessories or toiletries, or you could make shorter, wider ones to hang up next to bunk beds. If you switch the loops for ties, it can be attached to the end of a bed.

- For a simpler version, skip the binding and just hem the edges.

WALL POCKET TEMPLATES (⅕ actual size)

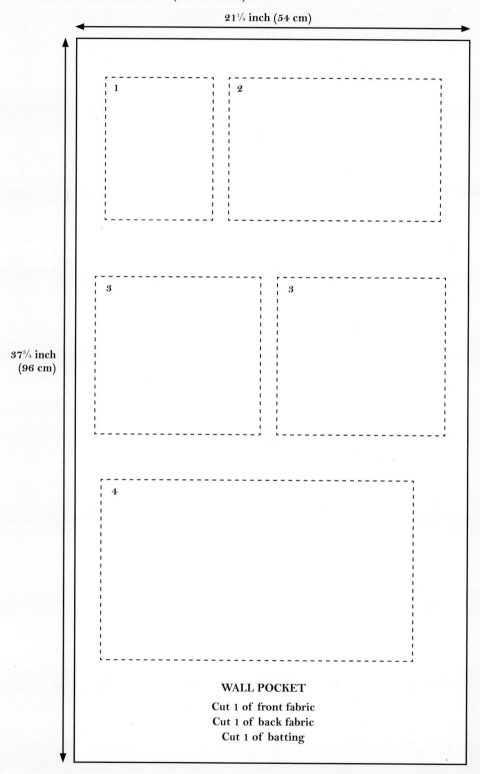

21¼ inch (54 cm)

37¾ inch (96 cm)

1

2

3

3

4

WALL POCKET

Cut 1 of front fabric
Cut 1 of back fabric
Cut 1 of batting

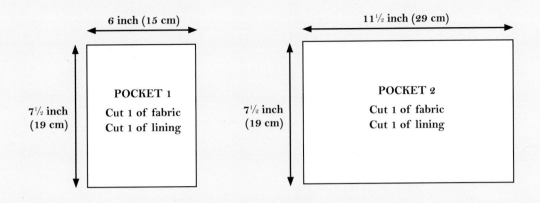

6 inch (15 cm)

POCKET 1
Cut 1 of fabric
Cut 1 of lining

7½ inch
(19 cm)

11½ inch (29 cm)

POCKET 2
Cut 1 of fabric
Cut 1 of lining

7½ inch
(19 cm)

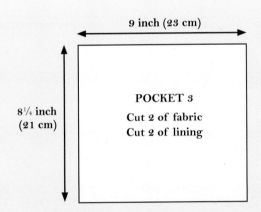

9 inch (23 cm)

POCKET 3
Cut 2 of fabric
Cut 2 of lining

8¼ inch
(21 cm)

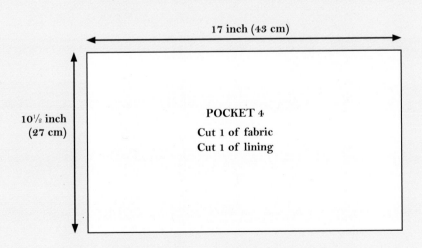

17 inch (43 cm)

POCKET 4
Cut 1 of fabric
Cut 1 of lining

10½ inch
(27 cm)

Further Ideas

Wall pockets work well for smaller toys, and pegboard is also useful for hanging larger sports equipment.

Tip

Visibility is essential when storing playthings, especially when you're in a hurry to get to sports events or parties and need to find things quickly.

Tip

Large sports equipment such as balls can be held in place using strong bungee cords stretched taut between two sturdy shelves.

Keep your antique toys and books together on display for all to enjoy.

Old fruit crates are
available from antique
stores and markets.
Use them for a touch
of vintage style.

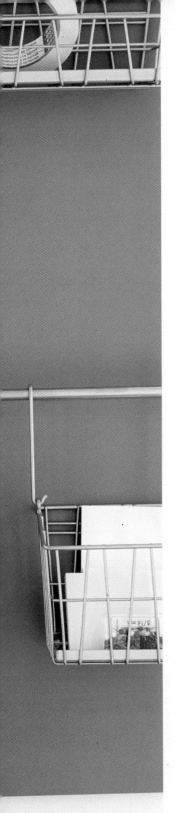

Chapter 7

HOME OFFICE & CRAFT ROOM

Whatever size your workspace is, keep it contained, organized and inspirational. There are lots of ways to hang, store and display essential items to ensure this room remains a happy place to work. Just remember to tidy away when you finish!

HOME OFFICE & CRAFT ROOM

A workspace can be anything from a small corner of the room to a large designated area. Either way, organization and some pretty storage is a good start.

Make use of wall space and add shelving above a desk. Crates or boxes can be really useful when wall-mounted as they serve as handy storage; paint the insides in bright shades for a color pop. If you use folders and box files, keep to the same colors or patterns for a neat look, and cover them with your favorite papers for a pretty finish. A few wooden clipboards hung on the wall can double up as inspiration boards.

Small drawers on wheels can sit underneath the desk, and put small boxes or cutlery trays in them to keep the drawers tidy. Keep pens and office supplies in pots to keep your work area clear. Pegboards are a versatile option for storage and display. If your workspace is used for crafting you could display your supplies in wire baskets or neat piles on a shelf for extra color and inspiration. Sewing machines can be bulky so have a cupboard or space they can be moved to when not in use, or use a pretty pillowcase to cover them. A large cupboard is useful for storing things like printers and inks, and add under-shelf baskets for holding spare paper.

Craft Case on page 127

Crafty Peg Board on page 130

Pen Pots

These customized, enamel camping mugs are ideal for storing pens, scissors or paintbrushes. The paper doilies are used for stencils as they give a geometric floral look, but you could just draw the patterns straight onto the mug. You can apply a coat of clear varnish to keep the patterns from wearing off.

TOOLS & MATERIALS

- 3 white or light-colored camping mugs
- Sharpie pens in various colors
- Paper lace doilies
- Pencil
- Clear acrylic spray varnish (optional)

1. Make sure the cups are clean and dry.
2. Using the pencil, lightly draw some guidelines directly onto the mug. Choose a pattern on the doily that will be suitable for a repeat floral motif and place flat onto the surface of the cup.
3. Working in a well-ventilated space and using your Sharpie pens, trace the shapes through the doily. Switch or add colors as you go, and don't worry if some of the flower shapes aren't too neat as you can go over them when you have finished.
4. Leave to dry before spraying with clear varnish.

Tips
- You could use these in other rooms such as the kitchen for storing cutlery or napkins.
- You can use porcelain pens or paints or even stickers. If you can't find this kind of mug you could use white china cups or plant pots.

Wall Box

This is an easy DIY project to make a display shelf that is perfect for storing sewing or craft supplies. It is made from a wooden cutlery tray that you can find in most kitchen shops. The best ones are those with three or four compartments, as when you flip it on its side these will become the shelves. This wall box has been painted but I have also added a bit of leftover fabric. The top has a couple of holes drilled in, so you can hang it with some cord. Small sample pots of paint are just the right size for decorating this shelf.

TOOLS & MATERIALS

- A wooden cutlery tray
- Sandpaper
- Paint in 3 or 4 colors
- Paintbrushes

- Fabric remnant
- Scissors
- PVA glue
- Drill

- A 11¾ inch (29.5 cm) length of brightly colored paracord or string

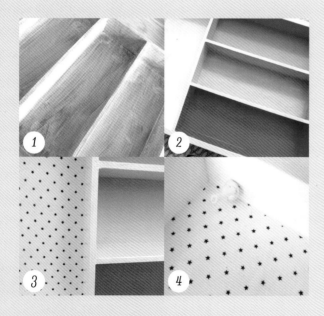

1. Lightly sand the wood ready to paint. Decide which way round you will be hanging the tray and drill a hole ¾ inch (2 cm) in from the edge on each side. Undercoat everything in white first to give a good color base.

2. Begin painting, allowing each color to dry in between coats. Use a small paintbrush to keep the lines between each color neat.

3. When all the paint is dry, measure and cut the fabric piece and glue down, smoothing out any creases.

4. When dry, thread the cord through the holes on the top and knot securely ready to hang.

Tips

- If you want to make a bigger version you could attach two trays together.

- Another way to hang the wall box would be to leave out the cord and just attach a small picture hanger to the back.

- These box shelves look cute in a child's room being used to display small toys or dolls' house furnishings.

Craft Case

This vanity case was found in a bit of a rough state, but with a little TLC it has been brought back to life. Now it is a handy carrier for supplies, making it perfect for a spot of portable crafting. Look out for old suitcases; even ratty ones can be useful for all sorts of organization. Small vanity-sized ones work best, and those with the harder shell are easier to work with. You will also need some lightweight oilcloth fabric, which can be sourced online.

TOOLS & MATERIALS

- A small suitcase
- A 39¼ inch (1 m) length of vinyl oilcloth fabric
- Scissors
- Craft knife
- Sewing machine
- Thread
- Pencil
- Measuring tape
- A 39¼ inch (1 m) length of bias binding
- Strong double-sided tape

1. To begin you will need to remove any lining the case already has. To do this, carefully cut away the lining with a craft knife.

2. To make the new lining, place the suitcase on top of the fabric and trace around the shape.

3. Cut out three pieces of this shape—one for the lid, base and the outer top. Take one of the cut pieces and place inside on the bottom of the case; it will be a little bit larger than you need so draw around the excess with a pencil.

4. Trim to size.

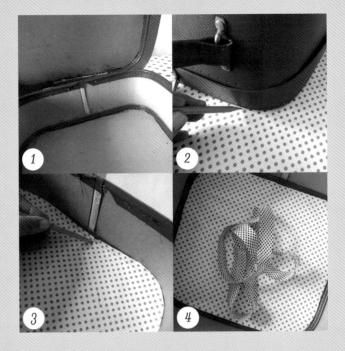

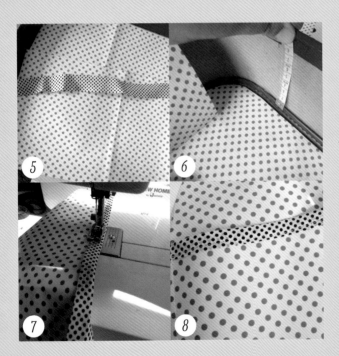

5. Repeat with the lid, using this piece as a template to cut out the pocket shape. This will need to be the same shape but approximately 4 inch (10 cm) shorter in height.

6. Measure around the sides of the case. Cut out a strip to fit the measurements and also a piece to cover the part where the lid joins the base.

7. Take a piece of binding and cut it just a little longer than the length of the pocket opening, fold in half and stitch to the pocket piece along the top edge.

8. Place together the lid piece and the pocket piece, both with right sides facing upward, fold in the excess binding and stitch together using a narrow seam.

9. Take the rest of the binding, fold in half and stitch down.

10. Fold in and stitch the raw edges at each end. Measure the center point of the base piece and of the binding. Stitch the binding onto the base piece in the center, and repeat at each side so the binding is secured down in three places. This makes the loops for holding notebooks or fabric.

11. The rest of the binding forms ties to hold things in place inside the suitcase.

12. Using the double-sided tape, stick down the join piece to the suitcase, then the base and top pieces.

13. Add the side piece and press down firmly to make sure the fabric is well stuck.

14. Finally, take the outer top piece and stick down with the double-sided tape. If your suitcase has piped edges you can push any excess fabric under the piping with a flat knife to give it a neater finish.

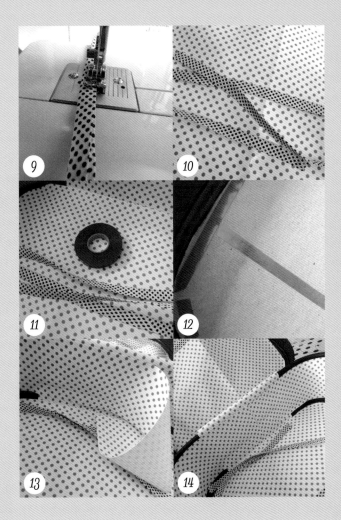

Tips

- You could line the inside and leave out the pocket if you prefer to just spruce up a suitcase.

- Depending on what you plan to keep in it, you could make smaller pockets for pens, or add pockets around the sides for sewing supplies.

- This suitcase would be great for a painter or knitter and would make a good gift for an organized crafter.

- If you are using it for crafts, keep spare equipment inside so you are always prepared.

Crafty Pegboard

This pegboard is so versatile, it can be changed and re-arranged to suit your style. The hardware fixings can be found in shop-fitting supply stores, or DIY stores where they will cut it to size. All you need is an old picture frame with the glass removed.

TOOLS & MATERIALS

- A medium to large picture frame, no back or glass needed
- Wooden pegboard, pre-cut to the internal measurement of the frame—if you are unsure, take the frame with you to the wood merchants
- Paint in 2 colors
- Paintbrushes
- Liquid nails or instant-grab adhesive
- 2 metal wallplates for attaching to the wall
- Pegboard hardware hooks and fixings

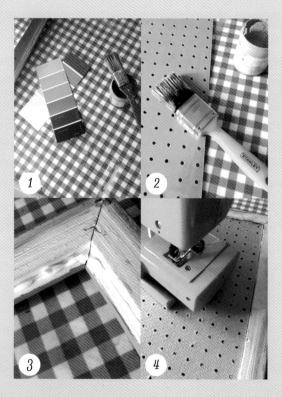

1. Make sure your frame is clean and dry. Paint it in your chosen color and leave to dry overnight. You may need to apply several coats for an even finish.

2. Paint the pegboard with your second color. Try not to load the brush with too much paint as it can run into the holes.

3. When both the frame and pegboard are dry, place the frame right side facing downward. Carefully apply the instant-grab adhesive all along the edges of the inside frame.

4. Place the pegboard right side facing down into the picture frame and press into place. If the adhesive escapes on the right side, wipe it before it dries. Place flat on a surface, right side down, and put a heavy item over the pegboard to help it stick.

5. Once the glue is dry, if you have any paint-blocked peg holes, push a small screwdriver or skewer into them and twist to open them up. Securely add the metal wallplates on the back of the frame ready for hanging. Start adding the pegboard hooks and gather your supplies ready to hang in place.

Tips

- You could make this in a much larger version as a door panel or part of a wall.

- If you can find it, Perspex pegboard is really cool and would work in just the same way.

- When buying supplies try to keep to a color or theme so when they are hanging on your pegboard they give a pretty look.

- These boards look good in other rooms too—in a kitchen to display and store favorite cups or in a garden shed to organize small tools and planting equipment.

Further Ideas

Personalize your box files using scraps of newsprint as labels.

A small metal tin is ideal for organizing and storing photographs. Use index cards to separate them into categories such as year, month, occasion.

Tip

Keeping your work space clear will ensure peace of mind and greater productivity. Keep it light, bright and cheerful to enable you to focus.

An oven shelf can be recycled into a handy pegboard.

Be prepared for important dates. Use a clear box file and some index cards, add greetings cards to the relevant sections, and store spare wrapping paper at the back. Clip a calendar onto the front.

Chargers and cables can all look very similar, so label them with washi tape. To keep them organized use metal clips attached to the desk and thread each cable through to keep it in place.

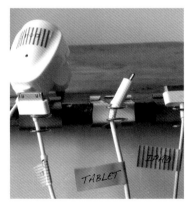

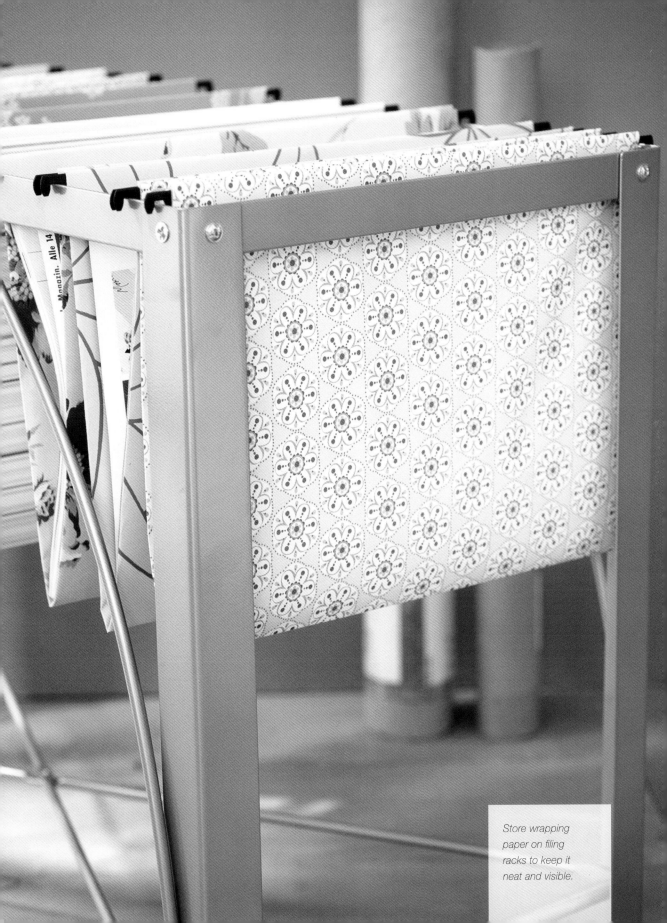

Store wrapping paper on filing racks to keep it neat and visible.

Chapter 8

OUTDOORS

This outdoor space, however big or small, is like another room in your home. Constantly evolving and changing, your yard needs a bit of TLC to keep it looking nice. Make over pots and garden tools with a lick of fresh paint and keep the flowers growing all summer long with some handy seed organization.

- Plant Hanger (page 137)

- Seed Organizer (page 138)

- Further Ideas (page 140)

OUTDOORS

A garden shed can be useful for storage and for outdoor jobs. Plan to keep one side especially for storing things like outdoor chairs or lawnmowers, etc. Use stackable plastic boxes or metal shelving for small outdoor toys such as bats and balls; label the boxes so you know where to find things and keep spare sticky labels and a marker pen on hand. Keep the other side of the shed clear for using as a work area. A small, narrow table is handy, and if you are short on space keep a flip-up one that will fold away when not in use. Hooks on the walls or hanging storage is perfect for small plants and tools. Narrow shelves are good for keeping all your seeds and pots in one place ready for planting-out season. Metal pails are handy for carrying your tools and equipment around the yard, and you can spray paint them any color to match your scheme.

Use the back of the shed door for extra hanging storage: add some coat pegs and you have somewhere to keep the gardening apron and gloves. Painted wooden crates can be used to hold paint cans and brushes. Label the lids so you know where each color was used in case of touch-ups. You can hang up your rubber boots using a trouser clip hanger; that way they are easy to find and the spiders can't crawl inside! If your shed has a window, add some pretty curtains. Keep the outside of the shed painted to protect the wood and re-apply every year before winter. If the inside is dark then paint it white; it really makes a difference. If your shed is off grid, solar-powered string lights are easy to fit and look so pretty at night.

Plant Hanger on page 137

You can paint large wooden popsicle sticks for plant labels, and garden canes strung with twine and fabric scraps are good for keeping birds away from seedlings.

Plant Hanger

This hanging storage is ideal for holding small plants like succulents or herbs and can be hung from a hook inside or out. The project requires a cheap shower caddy like those in which you store shampoo and soaps. They usually have a hanger shape at the top and come in different shapes and designs, but so long as the shape works for holding small to medium pots and plants it should be just fine. If you are going to hang it outside, make sure to use strong glue instead of double-sided tape to hold the yarn.

TOOLS & MATERIALS

- Metal shower caddy
- Spray paint
- Double-sided tape or glue
- Scissors
- Small amount of yarn in various colors

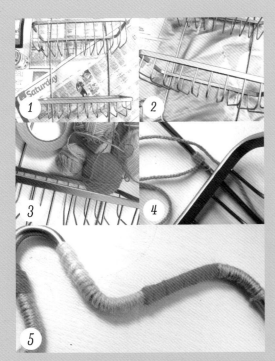

1. Make sure the caddy is clean and dry, and remove any soap residue as the paint will not cover this.

2. Take outside to spray two coats of paint, and avoid inhaling the fumes. Do one side at a time and allow each coat to dry thoroughly. Leave overnight.

3. To add the wraps of yarn, decide where the colors will go and how much you wish to add. Put a small strip of the double-sided tape at the start point.

4. Take the first color of yarn and stick the end onto the tape. Begin wrapping tightly around the caddy, making sure that all the metal underneath is covered and the yarn is neat and flat.

5. How much you wrap is up to you, but these stripes are approximately 1¼–2 inch (3–5 cm) wide. To finish each color, cut the yarn leaving some extra length and tie securely in a knot and trim. Begin the next color in the same way as before with the double-sided tape. Cover the end of the last color as you begin wrapping the new stripe. Trim off loose ends and stick down with glue. Line the basket before adding pots, and hang tools on the side.

Seed Organizer

Growing things can take a bit of organization and planning. This little tin will hold all your dried seeds ready for the next season, stored in sections for each month or time of year. This project uses a vintage candy tin as it is just the right size. My tin was very old and the design had worn off so I spray painted it first to neaten it up and removed the lid. You can use readymade envelopes for your seeds, but if you can't find these then you could adapt larger envelopes or make your own from tracing paper. The header sections are made from scrapbooking card and are custom made to fit the tin. Names of seeds can be written on the colored labels.

TOOLS & MATERIALS

- A medium-sized square or rectangular tin
- 6 sheets of scrapbooking card
- Paper envelopes
- Sewing machine and thread
- Scissors
- Pencil
- Ruler
- Assorted stickers

Make sure the tin is clean and dry. If yours has a nice design and is in good condition you can use it just as it is; if not, then you can paint or decorate it. For this project, as well as painting the tin, I raided the craft cupboard and added a ribbon and some floral letters.

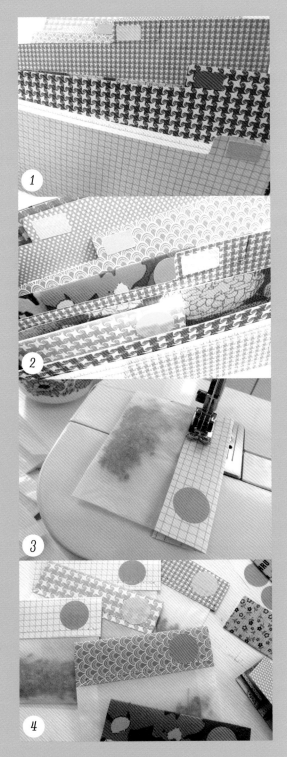

To make the index files

1. Measure the height and depth of the tin. Double the height measurement and add an extra ⅜ inch (1 cm) on top of that. Cut out six headers from your scrapbooking card using your measurements. Fold the card so that the front is ⅜ inch (1 cm) higher than the back to make the header tab, and cut away the tab shapes as shown to create an index style card. To get an idea of how big the tab should be, take your width measurement and divide by six.

2. Add stickers or labels to the tabs with months of the year and arrange them in your tin.

To make seed packets

3. With any spare card left over from your index files, cut rectangles that are the same width as your envelopes and approximately 1½ inch (4 cm) tall. Fold in half. Put your seeds into the envelopes, remembering to label the new envelopes with the contents and date as you go along. Fold over the top of the envelopes and add the folded card. Stitch the card and envelope together to secure. Add to the tin in the relevant section.

4. Use colored labels to identify different seed types.

Tips

- You can add index cards in each section and write any information you think will be handy as the plants grow so you are even more prepared for next year. Keep some spare envelopes and card on hand for any new seeds you want to add as the year goes on.

- You could staple the card tops onto the envelopes instead of stitching.

- Another option is to use a mini box file for this project and just customize it in your own style with fabric or stickers.

- Small money envelopes work well if you don't want to make the seed packets, and if you prefer to keep seeds in the dark try to find a tin with a lid.

Further Ideas

Tip

Use old pieces of furniture or crockery from inside the house to create repurposed containers and handy surface areas in your outdoor space.

This old cutlery drawer makes an excellent portable tool holder.

A wicker basket such as this one threaded with stiff material is the perfect container for all your garden tools and useful bits and pieces.

INDEX

ACKNOWLEDGMENTS

This is the bit where I get to say . . . Thank you, with all my heart.

To Rob for your unwavering support and love, and for telling me where to put full stops. I couldn't have done this without you at my side. To our brilliant boys Charlie and Ollie—you inspire me every day and make me smile. To Arnie, our little dog, for keeping me company when I worked late into the night. To my lovely Mum and Dad who showed me how to make and create, and to believe in myself.

To my family and friends who put up with my witterings and forgetfulness when deadlines were looming. To Emma for your support and inspirational friendship, as well as endless supplies of pep talks and tea, and for providing the odd items I struggled to find. To Jane for being such a lovely, thoughtful friend, as well as being the most organized (in a pretty way) person I know.

A big thank you to all the people at Quintet who worked on this book, especially Ellie for finding me, Emma, Ella and Michael. To Sussie Bell for taking such beautiful pictures. To Caroline for all your help and patience, and for making the first time I write a book not quite as scary as I thought it would be.

And last but not least to the readers, commenters and customers of *littleteawagon* and *teawagontales* for the support and friendship you guys have given me over the last few years . . . a great big THANK YOU X

PICTURE CREDITS

Key: l=left, r=right, c=center, t=top, b=bottom

Jesse Dresbach: 34l, 56br, 68r, 140tl, 140tr

© **GAP Interiors**: Tria Giovan 16; Costas Picadas 58; Ingrid Rasmussen 68l; Bruce Hemming 70; Dan Duchars 134

Jane Hughes: 11, 12t, 13, 34r, 39, 52, 56l, 56tr, 57, 60, 82t, 96b, 97, 118tr, 118br, 132tr, 132bl, 132bc, 140b, 143, 144 and all project step photography

© **living4media**: Franziska Taube 10b, 132tl; Winfried Heinze 10t, 69, 141; Simon Scarboro 12b; Julia Hoersch 35, 82br, 83, 120, 133; Gallo Images Pty Ltd. 68l; Sabine Löscher 82bl; Built Images 84; ETSA 96t, 101, People Pictures 118l Revier 51 119

© **Shutterstock**: Thomas Bethge 32; Triana Shiyan 98

All other photographs were taken by Sussie Bell and are copyright of Quintet Publishing Ltd.

Although every effort has been made to credit contributors, Quintet Publishing would like to apologize should there have been any omissions or errors, and would be pleased to make the appropriate correction for future editions of the book. Any trademarks are the property of their respective owners, none of whom are affiliated to or endorse this book.